The Formula of Wealth

The Formula of Wealth:
How to Create, Manage and Multiply Your Money

RIKROSES
BOOKS AND E-BOOKS

SUMMARY

INTRODUCTION

What is wealth? How can you create it, manage it and multiply it? How can you use it to improve your life and the lives of others? These are some of the questions that this book will answer for you.

This book is not a get-rich-quick scheme or a magic formula. It is a comprehensive guide to understanding the concept of wealth and its implications for your personal and professional success. It is based on scientific research, practical experience and timeless wisdom from various fields and disciplines. It will teach you the principles, practices and skills that will help you achieve your financial goals and live a fulfilling life.

This book is for anyone who wants to improve their financial situation and their quality of life. Whether you are a beginner or an expert, a student or a professional, an employee or an entrepreneur, a saver or an investor, a spender or a donor, this book will provide you with valuable information, advice and inspiration that will help you achieve your desired level of wealth.

This book is also for anyone who wants to understand the nature and role of wealth in our society. Whether you are interested in economics, politics, sociology, psychology, history, culture or spirituality, this book will offer you a comprehensive perspective on how wealth affects our lives individually and collectively.

This book is not only about money. It is about much more than that. It is about creating value, making a difference, living with purpose. It is about finding your formula of wealth.

Welcome to this journey. Let's begin.

CHAPTER 1: The Concept of Wealth and Why It Matters

What is wealth? How do you define it? How do you measure it? How do you create it? How do you manage it? How do you multiply it? These are some of the questions that this book will answer for you.

Wealth is not just about money. Money is only a tool, a means to an end. Wealth is about having the resources, the freedom, and the impact that you want in your life. Wealth is about living your purpose, fulfilling your potential, and making a difference in the world.

Wealth is not a fixed or finite quantity. Wealth is not a zero-sum game, where one person's gain is another person's loss. Wealth is not a privilege or a luck, reserved for a few or bestowed by chance. Wealth is a dynamic and abundant phenomenon, where one person's success can inspire and benefit many others. Wealth is a possibility and a responsibility, available to anyone and demanded by everyone.

Wealth is not a destination or a status. Wealth is not something that you achieve or attain once and for all. Wealth is not something that you have or own as a possession. Wealth is a journey and a process. Wealth is something that you create and cultivate as a skill. Wealth is something that you manage and multiply as a habit.

Wealth matters because it affects every aspect of your life. Your wealth determines your health, your happiness, your relationships, your opportunities, your choices, your actions, and your legacy. Your wealth influences your self-image, your self-esteem, your self-confidence, and your self-worth. Your wealth shapes your worldview, your values, your beliefs, and your principles.

6

Wealth matters because it reflects who you are, what you do, and how you live. Your wealth is an expression of your identity, your purpose, and your impact. Your wealth is a manifestation of your vision, your goals, and your dreams. Your wealth is a demonstration of your competence, your creativity, and your contribution.

Wealth matters because it empowers you to make a difference in the world. Your wealth enables you to solve problems, to create value, to serve others, and to make an impact. Your wealth allows you to support causes, to fund projects, to invest in opportunities, and to make a change. Your wealth helps you to leave a legacy, to inspire others, to empower generations, and to make a difference.

This book will teach you how to create, manage and multiply your wealth in every area of your life. You will learn the concept of wealth and why it matters. You will discover the four pillars of wealth creation: mindset, habits, skills, and strategies. You will master the tools of wealth: money management, investing, entrepreneurship, and personal branding. You will explore the risks of wealth: financial literacy, debt management, asset protection, and tax planning. You will understand the ethics of wealth: social responsibility, environmental sustainability, philanthropy, and generosity. You will develop the psychology of wealth: motivation, discipline, resilience, and gratitude. You will improve the relationships of wealth: networking, communication, collaboration, and mentorship. You will design the lifestyle of wealth: health, happiness, balance, and fulfillment. You will plan the legacy of wealth: vision, goals, action plans, and accountability.

This book will challenge you to think differently about wealth and to take action accordingly. This book will inspire you to pursue wealth not only as a personal goal but also as a global mission. This book will empower you to create wealth not only for yourself but also for others.

Are you ready to embark on this journey? Are you ready to unleash your potential? Are you ready to make a difference?

Let's begin.

7

CHAPTER 2: The Four Pillars of Wealth Creation

In this chapter, we will explore the four pillars of wealth creation, which are the essential elements that you need to master in order to build and grow your wealth. These four pillars are:

1) **Income:** The amount of money that you earn from your work, business, investments, or other sources. Income is the fuel that powers your wealth creation engine. Without income, you cannot save, invest, or spend money. Therefore, you need to increase your income as much as possible by developing your skills, expanding your network, creating value, solving problems, and seizing opportunities. You also need to diversify your income streams by having multiple sources of income, such as salary, bonuses, commissions, dividends, interest, royalties, rents, or profits. This way, you can reduce your risk and increase your stability and security.

2) **Expenses:** The amount of money that you spend on your living costs, taxes, debts, or other obligations. Expenses are the friction that slows down your wealth creation engine. With expenses, you lose money that could otherwise be used to grow your wealth. Therefore, you need to reduce your expenses as much as possible by living below your means, budgeting wisely, avoiding unnecessary spending, negotiating better deals, and minimizing taxes and fees. You also need to prioritize your expenses by focusing on the ones that are essential for your survival and well-being, such as food, shelter, health care, education, and insurance. This way, you can save more money and invest it for the future.

8

3) **Assets:** The things that you own that have value and can generate income or appreciate over time, such as real estate, stocks, bonds, businesses, or intellectual property. Assets are the vehicles that drive your wealth creation engine. With assets, you make money work for you instead of working for money. Therefore, you need to acquire more assets as much as possible by saving and investing your money in productive and profitable assets that match your goals, risk tolerance, time horizon, and interests. You also need to protect and maintain your assets by insuring them against losses or damages, diversifying them across different categories and markets, and optimizing their performance and returns. This way, you can increase your wealth over time and achieve financial freedom.

4) **Liabilities:** The things that you owe that have a negative impact on your wealth and can reduce your income or devalue your assets, such as mortgages, loans, credit cards, or lawsuits. Liabilities are the obstacles that block your wealth creation engine. With liabilities, you pay money to others instead of keeping it for yourself. Therefore, you need to eliminate or minimize your liabilities as much as possible by avoiding or reducing debt, paying off your debt as soon as possible with the highest interest rate first (debt avalanche method) or the smallest balance first (debt snowball method), using credit cards responsibly and paying them in full every month (or not using them at all), and staying out of legal trouble. You also need to manage your liabilities by understanding their terms and conditions (such as interest rates, fees, penalties, and deadlines), using them wisely and strategically (such as leveraging them to buy assets that generate more income than the cost of debt), and monitoring them regularly and diligently (such as checking your credit score and report and correcting any errors or frauds). This way, you can free up more money and use it to grow your wealth.

The key to wealth creation is to increase your income, reduce your expenses, acquire more assets, and eliminate or minimize your liabilities. By doing so, you will create a positive cash flow that will allow you to save and invest more money, which will in turn increase your wealth over time.

However, this is easier said than done. Many people struggle with managing their money and making smart financial decisions. They may have low or unstable income, high or unnecessary expenses, few or no assets, and many or large liabilities. They may also lack the knowledge, skills, habits, mindset, strategies, tools,

9

ethics, psychology, relationships, lifestyle, legacy, future vision, secrets, myths, opportunities, wisdom, and art of wealth creation that we will cover in the following chapters.

That is why it is important to understand the four pillars of wealth creation and how they affect your financial situation. You need to know where you stand in terms of your income, expenses, assets, and liabilities. You need to track and measure your financial performance and progress. You need to set realistic and specific goals for each pillar and create a plan to achieve them. You need to take action and implement the best practices and principles that we will share with you in this book.

In the next sections, we will explain each pillar in more detail and give you some tips and examples on how to improve them. We will also show you how to calculate your net worth, which is the difference between your assets and liabilities and a simple indicator of your wealth level. By the end of this chapter, you will have a clear picture of your current financial situation and a roadmap for creating more wealth in the future.

CHAPTER 3: The Mindset of Wealth

What is the difference between a wealthy person and a poor person? Is it the amount of money they have in their bank account, the assets they own, or the lifestyle they enjoy? While these are all indicators of wealth, they are not the root cause of it. The root cause of wealth is the mindset of the person who creates it.

The mindset of wealth is the way of thinking that enables a person to attract, create, manage and multiply money. It is the set of beliefs, attitudes, values and habits that shape how a person views money, wealth and success. It is the foundation of wealth creation, and without it, no amount of money, skills or strategies will make a person wealthy.

The mindset of wealth is not something that a person is born with or inherits from their parents. It is something that a person develops through education, experience and practice. It is something that a person can learn, change and improve at any stage of their life. It is something that a person can choose to adopt or reject.

The mindset of wealth has several characteristics that distinguish it from the mindset of poverty or scarcity. Some of these characteristics are:

- A wealthy mindset sees money as a tool, not a goal. Money is a means to an end, not an end in itself. Money is a way to achieve one's purpose, vision and values, not a measure of one's worth or happiness.
- A wealthy mindset sees money as abundant, not scarce. Money is everywhere, and there is enough for everyone. Money is constantly flowing and circulating, not static or fixed. Money is something to be created and shared, not hoarded or feared.
- A wealthy mindset sees money as an opportunity, not a problem. Money is a source of freedom, choice and possibility, not a source of stress,

11

worry or limitation. Money is something to be enjoyed and appreciated, not something to be avoided or resented.

- **A wealthy mindset sees money as a responsibility, not a right.** Money is a gift that comes with a duty to use it wisely, ethically and generously. Money is something to be earned and respected, not something to be taken for granted or abused.
- **A wealthy mindset sees money as a result, not a cause.** Money is an effect of one's actions, decisions and behaviors, not a cause of them. Money is a reflection of one's value creation, not a determinant of it.
- **A wealthy mindset sees money as a partner, not an enemy.** Money is a friend that supports one's goals and dreams, not a foe that opposes them. Money is something to be aligned with and leveraged, not something to be fought against or controlled.

These are some of the key aspects of the mindset of wealth that enable a person to create, manage and multiply their money. In this chapter, we will explore each of these aspects in more detail and provide some practical tips on how to develop them in your own life.

A wealthy mindset sees money as a tool, not a goal.

This means that you don't chase money for its own sake, but rather use it as a means to achieve your true purpose, vision and values. You don't let money define your success or happiness, but rather use it to support your personal growth and fulfillment. For example, instead of working for money, you work for your passion and mission. Instead of spending money on things that don't matter, you invest money on things that do matter. Instead of saving money for the sake of saving, you save money for the sake of living.

A wealthy mindset sees money as abundant, not scarce.

This means that you don't operate from a mentality of lack, but rather from a mentality of abundance. You don't see money as something that is limited or hard to get, but rather as something that is plentiful and easy to create. You don't hoard or fear money, but rather share and attract it. For example, instead of thinking that there is not enough money for everyone, you think that there is more than enough money for everyone. Instead of thinking that you have to compete for money, you think that you can cooperate for money. Instead of thinking that you have to work hard for money, you think that you can work smart for money.

A wealthy mindset sees money as an opportunity, not a problem.

12

This means that you don't view money as a source of stress, worry or limitation, but rather as a source of freedom, choice and possibility. You don't avoid or resent money, but rather enjoy and appreciate it. You don't see money as a problem to be solved, but rather as an opportunity to be seized. For example, instead of seeing money as a burden that weighs you down, you see money as a resource that lifts you up. Instead of seeing money as a constraint that holds you back, you see money as a tool that propels you forward. Instead of seeing money as a obstacle that blocks your way, you see money as a catalyst that sparks your creativity.

A wealthy mindset sees money as a responsibility, not a right.

This means that you don't take money for granted or abuse it, but rather respect and earn it. You don't see money as something that you are entitled to or deserve, but rather as something that you are gifted with and accountable for. You don't waste or misuse money, but rather use it wisely, ethically and generously. For example, instead of seeing money as something that you can spend without thinking, you see money as something that you can budget with planning. Instead of seeing money as something that you can use without caring, you see money as something that you can steward with integrity. Instead of seeing money as something that you can keep without sharing, you see money as something that you can give with gratitude.

A wealthy mindset sees money as a result, not a cause.

This means that you don't see money as a cause of your actions, decisions and behaviors, but rather as an effect of them. You don't see money as a determinant of your value creation, but rather as a reflection of it. You don't see money as something that happens to you, but rather as something that you make happen. For example, instead of seeing money as something that makes you do things, you see money as something that follows what you do. Instead of seeing money as something that measures your worth, you see money as something that mirrors your contribution. Instead of seeing money as something that controls your life, you see money as something that responds to your choices.

A wealthy mindset sees money as a partner, not an enemy.

This means that you don't see money as a friend or foe that supports or opposes your goals and dreams, but rather as a partner that works with you and for you. You don't fight against or control money, but rather align with and leverage it. You don't see money as something separate from you, but rather as something integrated with you. For example, instead of seeing money as something that competes with your

13

values, you see money as something that complements your values. Instead of seeing money as something that limits your potential, you see money as something that enhances your potential. Instead of seeing money as something that distracts from your purpose, you see money as something that supports your purpose.

14

CHAPTER 4: The Habits of Wealth

Wealth is not only a result of what you do, but also of how you do it. Your habits are the repeated actions that shape your behavior, your mindset, and your outcomes. In this chapter, we will explore the habits of wealth, the daily routines and practices that can help you create, manage and multiply your money.

The first habit of wealth is to have a clear vision of your financial goals. You need to know what you want to achieve, why you want to achieve it, and how you will measure your progress. Having a clear vision will help you stay focused, motivated, and aligned with your purpose. A vision is not a vague wish or a fantasy, but a realistic and specific plan that you can break down into smaller steps and actions.

The second habit of wealth is to budget your income and expenses. You need to know how much money you earn, how much money you spend, and how much money you save or invest. Budgeting will help you control your cash flow, avoid unnecessary debt, and allocate your resources wisely. A budget is not a restriction or a limitation, but a tool that helps you optimize your financial decisions and achieve your goals faster.

The third habit of wealth is to save and invest regularly. You need to set aside a portion of your income every month for your future needs and wants. Saving will help you build an emergency fund, prepare for unexpected events, and take advantage of opportunities. Investing will help you grow your money over time, generate passive income, and beat inflation. Saving and investing are not sacrifices or losses, but investments in yourself and your future.

The fourth habit of wealth is to diversify your income sources. You need to have more than one way of earning money, preferably from different industries, markets, and asset classes. Diversifying your income will help you reduce your risk, increase

15

your resilience, and multiply your potential returns. Diversification is not a complication or a distraction, but a strategy that helps you leverage your skills, knowledge, and network.

The fifth habit of wealth is to educate yourself constantly. You need to keep learning new things, updating your skills, and expanding your knowledge. Educating yourself will help you stay relevant, competitive, and valuable in the changing world. Education is not a cost or a burden, but an investment that pays dividends for life.

The sixth habit of wealth is to seek advice from experts. You need to consult with people who have more experience, knowledge, and success than you in the areas that matter to you. Seeking advice will help you avoid mistakes, learn from best practices, and accelerate your results. Advice is not a sign of weakness or ignorance, but a sign of wisdom and humility.

The seventh habit of wealth is to review and improve your performance. You need to track your results, analyze your data, and evaluate your progress. Reviewing and improving your performance will help you identify what works and what doesn't work for you, what strengths and weaknesses you have, and what opportunities and threats you face. Reviewing and improving are not chores or punishments, but opportunities to learn and grow.

These are the habits of wealth that can help you create, manage and multiply your money. They are not secrets or shortcuts, but proven principles that work for anyone who applies them consistently. By adopting these habits, you will not only improve your financial situation, but also enhance your personal development, happiness, and fulfillment.

CHAPTER 5: The Skills of Wealth

In this chapter, we will explore the skills that are essential for creating, managing and multiplying your money. These skills are not only useful for your financial success, but also for your personal and professional growth. By developing these skills, you will be able to achieve your goals faster, overcome challenges easier, and enjoy more fulfillment and satisfaction in life.

The skills of wealth are divided into three categories: technical skills, interpersonal skills and intrapersonal skills. Technical skills are the ones that relate to your specific field of expertise, such as accounting, marketing, engineering, etc. Interpersonal skills are the ones that help you communicate, collaborate and influence others effectively, such as listening, negotiating, persuading, etc. Intrapersonal skills are the ones that help you manage yourself better, such as self-awareness, self-regulation, self-motivation, etc.

Let's look at each category in more detail and see how you can improve them.

Technical Skills

Technical skills are the foundation of your wealth creation. They are the ones that allow you to provide value to the market and earn income from your work or business. Without technical skills, you will have a hard time finding or creating opportunities to make money.

Technical skills vary depending on your industry, profession or niche. For example, if you are a lawyer, you need to have legal knowledge and skills. If you are a programmer, you need to have coding knowledge and skills. If you are a writer, you need to have writing knowledge and skills.

17

The good news is that technical skills can be learned and improved through education, training and practice. You can enroll in courses, read books, watch videos, attend seminars, join workshops or hire coaches or mentors to help you acquire or enhance your technical skills. You can also learn from your peers, colleagues or competitors by observing their work or asking for feedback.

The key to mastering technical skills is to be curious, passionate and persistent. You need to have a strong desire to learn new things and improve your existing ones. You need to be willing to invest time, money and energy into your learning process. You need to be open to feedback and criticism and use them as opportunities to grow. You need to practice your skills regularly and apply them in real situations.

Interpersonal Skills

Interpersonal skills are the set of skills we use to interact and communicate with others. They are essential for building and maintaining positive relationships in our personal and professional lives. According to Indeed.com, some examples of interpersonal skills include active listening, teamwork, responsibility, dependability, leadership, motivation, flexibility, patience and empathy [1]. These skills help us to understand other people's perspectives, cooperate effectively, resolve conflicts and achieve our goals.

Interpersonal skills can be improved through practice, feedback and reflection. Some ways to improve interpersonal skills are:

- Practicing active listening by paying attention, asking questions and summarizing what the speaker said
- Giving and receiving constructive feedback by being specific, positive and respectful
- Expressing appreciation and gratitude to others by saying thank you, giving compliments and acknowledging their contributions
- Showing empathy and compassion to others by acknowledging their feelings, offering support and avoiding judgment
- Respecting diversity and inclusion by being aware of cultural differences, avoiding stereotypes and embracing different perspectives
- Developing emotional intelligence by recognizing, managing and expressing your own emotions appropriately
- Communicating clearly and assertively by using simple, direct and respectful language, avoiding jargon and slang

18

- Negotiating and compromising by finding common ground, offering solutions and respecting boundaries
- Collaborating and cooperating by sharing ideas, resources and responsibilities, being flexible and adaptable
- Leading and motivating others by setting clear goals, providing guidance and feedback, inspiring trust and confidence

Interpersonal skills are valuable for any career path, as they help us to work well with others, create positive work environments and achieve success. By improving our interpersonal skills, we can enhance our personal and professional relationships, increase our productivity and satisfaction, and contribute to our well-being and happiness.

Intrapersonal skills

Intrapersonal skills are the abilities that help a person to understand themselves, manage their emotions, cope with stress, and achieve their goals. They are also known as self-awareness skills, because they involve being aware of one's own strengths, weaknesses, preferences, values, and motivations. Intrapersonal skills are important for personal and professional development, as they can enhance one's self-confidence, self-esteem, self-regulation, and resilience. Some examples of intrapersonal skills are:

- **Self-reflection:** The ability to examine one's own thoughts, feelings, and actions, and learn from them.
- **Self-control:** The ability to regulate one's impulses, emotions, and behaviors, and resist temptations or distractions.
- **Self-motivation:** The ability to initiate and sustain one's own actions toward a desired outcome, without relying on external rewards or pressures.
- **Self-criticism:** The ability to evaluate one's own performance, identify areas of improvement, and seek feedback or guidance.
- **Self-expression:** The ability to communicate one's own ideas, opinions, and emotions in an appropriate and effective way.

Intrapersonal skills can be improved by practicing various techniques, such as:

- **Meditation:** A practice that involves focusing one's attention on a single object, thought, or sensation, and observing one's own mental processes.
- **Journaling:** A practice that involves writing down one's thoughts, feelings, and experiences on a regular basis, and reflecting on them.

19

- **Goal-setting:** A process that involves defining specific, measurable, achievable, relevant, and time-bound objectives for oneself, and tracking one's progress.
- **Affirmations:** A technique that involves repeating positive statements to oneself, such as "I am capable", "I am worthy", or "I can do this".
- **Visualization:** A technique that involves imagining oneself in a desired situation or outcome, and feeling the associated emotions.

Intrapersonal skills are essential for anyone who wants to grow as a person and achieve their full potential. By developing these skills, one can gain a better understanding of themselves and their purpose in life.

20

CHAPTER 6: The Strategies of Wealth

In the previous chapters, we have discussed the concept, the pillars, the mindset, the habits and the skills of wealth. In this chapter, we will explore the strategies of wealth, which are the methods and techniques that you can use to create, manage and multiply your money.

The strategies of wealth are not fixed or universal. They depend on your personal goals, preferences, risk tolerance, time horizon and resources. However, there are some general principles and guidelines that can help you choose and implement the best strategies for your situation.

The first principle is to diversify your income sources. This means that you should not rely on a single source of income, such as your salary, your business or your investments. Instead, you should have multiple streams of income that can provide you with stability, security and growth potential. For example, you can have income from your job, your side hustle, your rental properties, your dividends, your royalties, your online courses, etc. The more income sources you have, the less vulnerable you are to economic downturns, market fluctuations or unexpected events.

The second principle is to optimize your expenses. This means that you should spend less than you earn, and use the difference to save and invest. However, this does not mean that you should live frugally or deprive yourself of the things that you enjoy. Rather, it means that you should be mindful of your spending habits and prioritize your needs over your wants. You should also look for ways to reduce your fixed expenses, such as housing, transportation, utilities and insurance. By optimizing your expenses, you can increase your cash flow and build your wealth faster.

21

The third principle is to leverage your assets. This means that you should use the resources that you already have to generate more income or value. For example, you can leverage your knowledge and skills by creating a product or service that solves a problem or meets a demand. You can leverage your network and connections by finding partners, clients or mentors who can support your goals. You can leverage your money by borrowing at a low interest rate and investing at a high return rate. By leveraging your assets, you can amplify your results and accelerate your wealth creation.

The fourth principle is to automate your finances. This means that you should set up systems and processes that can handle your money matters without requiring much effort or attention from you. For example, you can automate your savings by setting up a direct deposit from your paycheck to your savings account. You can automate your investments by using a robo-advisor or a target-date fund that can adjust your portfolio according to your risk profile and time horizon. You can automate your bills by setting up recurring payments from your checking account or credit card. By automating your finances, you can simplify your life and avoid human errors or emotions that can interfere with your decisions.

The fifth principle is to educate yourself constantly. This means that you should never stop learning and improving your financial literacy and skills. You should always seek new information, insights and opportunities that can help you grow your wealth and achieve your goals. You should also be aware of the trends, changes and challenges that affect the economy, the markets and the society. You should read books, listen to podcasts, watch videos, attend seminars, join communities and consult experts that can teach you something valuable or inspire you to take action. By educating yourself constantly, you can stay ahead of the curve and adapt to any situation.

These are some of the strategies of wealth that you can apply to create, manage and multiply your money. However, remember that these are not the only strategies available or suitable for everyone. You should always do your own research, analysis and evaluation before choosing and implementing any strategy. You should also monitor and review your progress regularly and make adjustments as needed. Ultimately, the best strategy is the one that works for you.

CHAPTER 7: The Tools of Wealth

In this chapter, we will explore the tools of wealth, which are the practical and tangible resources that you can use to create, manage and multiply your money. These tools include:

Financial literacy: the ability to understand and apply financial concepts and principles, such as budgeting, saving, investing, borrowing, taxation, etc. Financial literacy is essential for wealth creation because it helps you to make informed and rational decisions about your money, avoid financial mistakes and scams, and take advantage of financial opportunities. For example, if you know how to budget, you can control your spending and save more money for your goals. If you know how to invest, you can grow your money faster and achieve financial freedom sooner. If you know how to borrow, you can use debt wisely and avoid paying unnecessary interest. If you know how to pay taxes, you can minimize your tax liability and maximize your after-tax income.

- Financial planning: the process of setting and achieving financial goals, based on your current situation, needs, preferences and future expectations. Financial planning is essential for wealth creation because it helps you to define your vision and values, align your actions with your purpose, and measure your progress and results. For example, if you have a clear vision of what you want to achieve in life, you can set specific and realistic financial goals that support your vision. If you have a clear set of values that guide your decisions, you can choose financial strategies that match your values. If you have a clear way of measuring your progress and results, you can track your performance and adjust your plan accordingly.

- Financial systems: the structures and mechanisms that facilitate the flow of money in the economy, such as banks, markets, currencies, regulations,

23

etc. Financial systems are essential for wealth creation because they provide the infrastructure and environment for financial transactions and activities. For example, if you have access to a reliable and efficient banking system, you can store, transfer and access your money safely and conveniently. If you have access to a diverse and liquid market system, you can buy and sell financial assets easily and profitably. If you have access to a stable and strong currency system, you can preserve the value of your money and avoid inflation. If you have access to a fair and transparent regulatory system, you can protect your rights and interests as a financial consumer.

- **Financial products**: the instruments and services that enable you to save, invest, borrow or transfer money, such as accounts, cards, loans, stocks, bonds, funds, etc. Financial products are essential for wealth creation because they offer the means and opportunities for financial growth and diversification. For example, if you have access to a variety of saving products, such as savings accounts, certificates of deposit or money market funds, you can earn interest on your money and build your wealth gradually. If you have access to a variety of investing products, such as stocks, bonds or mutual funds, you can generate returns on your money and build your wealth faster. If you have access to a variety of borrowing products, such as loans or credit cards, you can leverage other people's money and build your wealth strategically. If you have access to a variety of transferring products, such as wire transfers or mobile payments, you can send or receive money and build your wealth globally.

- **Financial technology**: the innovation and application of technology to improve the efficiency and accessibility of financial systems and products, such as online platforms, mobile apps, blockchain, artificial intelligence, etc. Financial technology is essential for wealth creation because it enhances your financial capabilities and opportunities. For example, if you have access to online platforms, such as websites or blogs, you can learn more about finance and share your knowledge with others. If you have access to mobile apps, such as banking or investing apps, you can manage your money anytime and anywhere. If you have access to blockchain technology, such as cryptocurrencies or smart contracts, you can participate in decentralized and secure financial transactions and activities. If you have access to artificial intelligence technology, such as robo-advisors or chatbots, you can get personalized and automated financial advice and assistance.

Each of these tools has its own advantages and disadvantages, benefits and costs, opportunities and risks. Therefore, it is important to learn how to use them wisely

24

and effectively, according to your financial goals and strategies. In this chapter, we will cover the following topics:

- How to develop your financial literacy and why it is essential for wealth creation
- How to create a financial plan that aligns with your vision and values
- How to navigate the financial systems and understand their impact on your wealth
- How to choose the best financial products for your needs and preferences
- How to leverage the financial technology to enhance your financial capabilities
- and opportunities

By the end of this chapter, you will have a better understanding of the tools of wealth and how to use them to your advantage. You will also learn some tips and tricks to optimize your financial performance and avoid common pitfalls.

Let's get started!

How to develop your financial literacy and why it is essential for wealth creation

Financial literacy is the ability to understand and use various financial skills, such as budgeting, saving, investing, and managing debt. It is essential for wealth creation because it helps people make smart decisions with their money and achieve their financial goals. Here are some ways to develop financial literacy and why they are important:

- **Create a budget:** A budget is a plan that shows how much money you have, how much you spend, and how much you save. It helps you track your income and expenses, identify your needs and wants, and prioritize your spending. A budget can also help you avoid overspending, reduce debt, and save for emergencies or future goals.

- **Pay yourself first:** This means setting aside a portion of your income for savings or investments before you pay your bills or spend on other things. Paying yourself first can help you build wealth over time by taking advantage of compound interest, which is the interest earned on your initial investment plus the interest earned on the interest. Paying yourself first can also help

25

you prepare for unexpected expenses or opportunities, such as a medical emergency or a business venture.

- **Pay bills promptly:** Paying your bills on time can help you avoid late fees, penalties, and interest charges, which can add up and hurt your credit score. A good credit score can help you qualify for better interest rates and terms when you borrow money, such as for a mortgage or a car loan. A good credit score can also affect other aspects of your life, such as renting an apartment, getting a job, or obtaining insurance.

- **Get your credit report:** A credit report is a record of your credit history, which shows how you have used credit in the past. It includes information such as your personal details, credit accounts, payment history, inquiries, and public records. You can get a free copy of your credit report from each of the three major credit bureaus (Equifax, Experian, and TransUnion) once every 12 months at www.annualcreditreport.com. You should check your credit report regularly to make sure it is accurate and to spot any signs of identity theft or fraud.

- **Check your credit score:** A credit score is a number that summarizes your credit risk based on the information in your credit report. It ranges from 300 to 850, with higher scores indicating lower risk. Your credit score can affect your ability to get credit, as well as the interest rate and terms you are offered. You can check your credit score for free from various sources, such as your bank, credit card issuer, or online service. You should monitor your credit score periodically to see how it changes over time and to learn how to improve it.

- **Manage debt:** Debt is money that you owe to someone else, such as a bank, a credit card company, or a friend. Debt can be useful when used wisely, such as to buy a home, start a business, or pay for education. However, debt can also be harmful when used unwisely, such as to buy things you don't need or can't afford. Debt can cost you money in interest and fees, reduce your cash flow and savings, and damage your credit score. You should manage your debt by paying more than the minimum amount due each month, paying off high-interest debt first, avoiding unnecessary debt, and seeking help if you are struggling with debt.

- **Invest in your future:** Investing is putting your money to work for you by buying assets that can generate income or appreciate in value over time.

26

Investing can help you grow your wealth faster than saving alone and achieve long-term goals such as retirement or college education. Investing can also help you beat inflation, which is the rise in the prices of goods and services over time. You should invest in your future by learning about different types of investments, such as stocks, bonds, mutual funds, real estate, etc., diversifying your portfolio across different asset classes and risk levels, and investing regularly and consistently over time.

How to create a financial plan that aligns with your vision and values

Creating a financial plan that aligns with your vision and values is not only possible, but also essential for achieving your goals and living a fulfilling life. A financial plan is more than just a budget or a savings strategy; it is a roadmap that reflects your personal and professional aspirations, as well as your core values and beliefs. Here are some steps to help you create a financial plan that aligns with your vision and values.

1) **Define your vision and values.** What are the things that matter most to you in life? What are your passions, dreams, and purpose? What are the principles and standards that guide your decisions and actions? Write down your vision and values in a clear and concise way, and use them as the foundation of your financial plan.

2) **Assess your current financial situation.** How much income do you earn, and how much do you spend? What are your assets and liabilities? What are your sources of income and expenses? How much do you save and invest? How much debt do you have, and what is the interest rate? How much risk can you tolerate, and what is your time horizon? Analyze your financial situation objectively, and identify your strengths and weaknesses.

3) **Set SMART goals.** SMART stands for Specific, Measurable, Achievable, Relevant, and Time-bound. Based on your vision and values, set SMART goals that reflect what you want to accomplish financially in the short-term, medium-term, and long-term. For example, a short-term goal could be to pay off a credit card debt in six months; a medium-term goal could be to save for a vacation in two years; and a long-term goal could be to retire comfortably at 65.

4) **Create a realistic budget.** A budget is a tool that helps you track your income and expenses, and allocate your money according to your priorities. A realistic budget should be based on your actual income and expenses, not

27

on your wishes or assumptions. It should also include categories for savings, investments, debt repayment, emergencies, and fun. A budget should be flexible enough to accommodate changes in your circumstances, but also disciplined enough to help you stick to your plan.

5) **Implement your plan and monitor your progress.** Once you have a budget, you need to put it into action and follow it consistently. You also need to monitor your progress regularly, and measure it against your goals. You can use various tools and apps to help you track your income, expenses, savings, investments, debt, net worth, and cash flow. You can also review your plan periodically, and make adjustments as needed to reflect changes in your vision, values, goals, or situation.

How to navigate the financial systems and understand their impact on your wealth

The financial systems are complex and often opaque, but they have a significant impact on your wealth and well-being. Understanding how they work and how to navigate them can help you make better financial decisions and achieve your goals. Here are some tips on how to do that:

- **Learn the basics of financial literacy.** Financial literacy is the ability to understand and use various financial concepts, such as budgeting, saving, investing, borrowing, and managing risk. It can help you plan for your future, avoid costly mistakes, and take advantage of opportunities. You can find many online resources, books, podcasts, and courses that can teach you the fundamentals of financial literacy.

- **Know your financial situation and goals.** Before you can navigate the financial systems, you need to know where you are and where you want to go. You should have a clear picture of your income, expenses, assets, liabilities, net worth, and cash flow. You should also have specific and realistic financial goals, such as saving for retirement, buying a house, or paying off debt. You can use tools like spreadsheets, apps, or financial planners to help you track and manage your finances.

- **Choose the right financial products and services.** The financial systems offer a variety of products and services that can help you achieve your goals, such as bank accounts, credit cards, loans, insurance, investments, and retirement plans. However, not all of them are suitable for your needs and

28

preferences. You should compare the features, benefits, costs, risks, and returns of different options and choose the ones that match your situation and goals. You should also read the fine print and understand the terms and conditions before signing any contracts or agreements.

- **Seek professional advice when needed.** The financial systems can be confusing and overwhelming, especially if you face complex or unfamiliar situations. You may need professional advice from experts who can guide you through the process and help you avoid pitfalls. For example, you may need a financial advisor if you want to create a comprehensive financial plan, an accountant if you need to file taxes or deal with audits, or a lawyer if you need to draft a will or deal with legal disputes. You should look for qualified, reputable, and trustworthy professionals who have your best interests at heart.

- **Stay informed and updated.** The financial systems are constantly changing and evolving due to factors such as technology, regulation, competition, innovation, and market conditions. You should stay informed and updated on the latest trends, developments, news, and opportunities that affect your finances. You can use sources like websites, blogs, newsletters, podcasts, magazines, newspapers, or TV shows that cover financial topics. You should also review your financial situation and goals regularly and adjust your strategies accordingly.

How to choose the best financial products for your needs and preferences

Choosing the best financial products for your needs and preferences can be a daunting task, especially with so many options available in the market. However, by following some simple steps and guidelines, you can make informed and smart decisions that suit your goals and circumstances.

The first step is to identify your financial needs and preferences. What are you saving or investing for? How much risk are you willing to take? How long do you plan to keep your money in the product? How much liquidity do you need? How much fees are you willing to pay? These are some of the questions that can help you narrow down your choices and find the products that match your criteria.

The second step is to compare different products and providers. You can use online tools and platforms, such as comparison websites, calculators, reviews, ratings, etc., to compare the features, benefits, costs, performance, reputation, and customer service of various financial products and providers. You can also consult with

29

financial advisors, experts, or friends who have experience with the products you are interested in.

The third step is to evaluate the pros and cons of each product and provider. You should weigh the advantages and disadvantages of each option carefully and objectively. You should also consider the trade-offs and opportunity costs involved. For example, if you choose a product that offers higher returns but higher risk, you may lose some or all of your money if the market goes down. If you choose a product that offers lower returns but lower risk, you may miss out on some potential gains if the market goes up.

The fourth step is to make a decision and take action. Once you have done your research and analysis, you should choose the product and provider that best meets your needs and preferences. You should also read the terms and conditions carefully before signing any contract or agreement. You should also monitor your product regularly and review it periodically to see if it still suits your changing goals and circumstances.

By following these steps, you can choose the best financial products for your needs and preferences. Remember that there is no one-size-fits-all solution when it comes to financial products. You should always do your own due diligence and seek professional advice if needed.

How to leverage the financial technology to enhance your financial capabilities and opportunities

Financial technology, or fintech, is the use of digital tools and platforms to provide financial services and products. Fintech can help you enhance your financial capabilities and opportunities in various ways, such as:

- Saving and investing: Fintech apps and websites can help you manage your money, track your expenses, set financial goals, and automate your savings. Some examples are Mint, Acorns, and Digit. You can also use fintech platforms to access different investment options, such as stocks, bonds, cryptocurrencies, peer-to-peer lending, and crowdfunding. Some examples are Robinhood, Coinbase, LendingClub, and Kickstarter.

- Borrowing and paying: Fintech can help you access credit and loans faster and easier than traditional banks. You can use fintech platforms to compare interest rates, terms, and fees, and apply for loans online. Some examples

30

are SoFi, Kabbage, and Affirm. You can also use fintech to make payments more convenient and secure, such as using mobile wallets, QR codes, biometrics, and contactless cards. Some examples are PayPal, Venmo, Apple Pay, and Google Pay.

- **Learning and earning:** Fintech can help you improve your financial literacy and skills through online courses, podcasts, blogs, newsletters, and videos. You can learn about topics such as budgeting, investing, taxes, retirement planning, and more. Some examples are Khan Academy, NerdWallet, The Balance, and Investopedia. You can also use fintech to earn extra income or start a business online. You can sell your products or services on e-commerce platforms, offer your skills or expertise on freelance platforms, or create and monetize your content on social media platforms. Some examples are Shopify, Etsy, Upwork, Fiverr, YouTube, and Patreon.

You can leverage fintech to enhance your financial capabilities and opportunities by using these digital tools and platforms to save and invest your money wisely, borrow and pay your debts efficiently, learn and earn more income creatively.

31

CHAPTER 8: The Risks of Wealth

Wealth is not a guarantee of happiness, security, or freedom. Wealth comes with its own set of challenges, dangers, and pitfalls that can undermine your success, well-being, and legacy. In this chapter, we will explore some of the most common risks of wealth and how to avoid or mitigate them.

One of the biggest risks of wealth is losing it. Whether due to market fluctuations, economic downturns, fraud, lawsuits, taxes, inflation, or bad decisions, wealth can be eroded or wiped out in a matter of days, months, or years. To protect your wealth, you need to diversify your assets, invest wisely, hedge against risks, plan for contingencies, and seek professional advice.

Another risk of wealth is becoming complacent. When you have achieved a certain level of wealth, you may feel that you have nothing more to strive for, learn from, or improve on. You may stop challenging yourself, growing your skills, or pursuing your passions. You may lose your motivation, creativity, or curiosity. To prevent this, you need to set new goals, seek new experiences, learn new things, and find new ways to contribute.

A third risk of wealth is becoming isolated. Wealth can create a distance between you and others who may not share your lifestyle, values, or interests. You may find it hard to relate to people who have different problems, perspectives, or priorities. You may lose touch with your friends, family, or community. You may also attract people who are only interested in your money, not in you as a person. To avoid this, you need to maintain your social connections, cultivate genuine relationships, and be generous and humble.

A fourth risk of wealth is becoming arrogant. Wealth can inflate your ego and make you feel superior to others who have less than you. You may develop a sense of

32

entitlement, privilege, or invincibility. You may disregard the rules, norms, or ethics that apply to others. You may disrespect or exploit people who work for you or depend on you. You may also lose sight of the sources and purposes of your wealth. To overcome this, you need to remember your roots, acknowledge your luck, appreciate your mentors, and honor your responsibilities.

A fifth risk of wealth is becoming addicted. Wealth can become an obsession that consumes your time, energy, and attention. You may constantly chase more money, more possessions, more status, or more power. You may neglect your health, happiness, or harmony. You may sacrifice your values, principles, or integrity. You may also miss out on the joys and meanings of life that money cannot buy. To break this cycle, you need to balance your work and life, prioritize your needs and wants, practice gratitude and contentment, and find fulfillment beyond wealth.

These are some of the risks of wealth that you need to be aware of and prepared for. Wealth is not a destination but a journey that requires constant vigilance and adjustment. By understanding the risks of wealth and how to manage them effectively, you can enjoy the benefits of wealth without suffering the costs.

CHAPTER 9: The Ethics of Wealth

Wealth is not only a matter of numbers, but also a matter of values. How you create, manage and multiply your money reflects who you are as a person, what you stand for and what you care about. In this chapter, we will explore the ethical aspects of wealth and how they can affect your financial success and happiness.

Ethics is the branch of philosophy that deals with moral principles and judgments. It is concerned with what is right and wrong, good and bad, fair and unfair in human conduct. Ethics can also be defined as the rules or standards that govern the behavior of individuals or groups in a given context or situation.

Ethics can be applied to any domain of human activity, including wealth creation. In fact, ethics is especially relevant for wealth creation, because money is a powerful tool that can be used for good or evil, for yourself or others, for now or later. Money can also influence your character, your relationships and your impact on the world.

Therefore, it is important to have a clear and consistent ethical framework that guides your decisions and actions regarding money. This framework should be based on your personal values, beliefs and goals, as well as the universal principles of justice, honesty, responsibility and respect. It should also take into account the consequences of your choices for yourself and others, both in the short and long term.

Having an ethical framework for wealth creation can help you:

- Align your financial goals with your life purpose and vision
- Avoid or resolve conflicts of interest and dilemmas that may arise in your financial dealings

34

- Enhance your reputation and credibility as a trustworthy and reliable person
- Build positive and lasting relationships with your partners, clients, employees, suppliers, investors and stakeholders
- Contribute to the common good and make a positive difference in the world
- Enjoy peace of mind and satisfaction from knowing that you are doing the right thing

In this chapter, we will discuss some of the key ethical issues that you may encounter in your journey to wealth creation. We will also provide some practical tips and examples on how to deal with them in an ethical manner. These issues include:

- How to define and measure wealth
- How to earn money ethically
- How to spend money ethically
- How to save money ethically
- How to invest money ethically
- How to donate money ethically
- How to manage money ethically

By the end of this chapter, you will have a better understanding of the ethics of wealth and how to apply them in your own financial life. You will also be able to recognize and avoid some of the common ethical pitfalls that can derail your wealth creation efforts. You will be able to create, manage and multiply your money in a way that is consistent with your values, principles and goals, and that brings you joy, fulfillment and meaning.

How to define and measure wealth

Wealth is a complex and multidimensional concept that can be defined and measured in different ways. One common way to define wealth is the total value of all the assets that a person or a group owns, minus their liabilities. This is also known as net worth. However, this definition does not capture other aspects of wealth, such as human capital, social capital, natural capital, or cultural capital. These are intangible forms of wealth that can enhance the well-being and productivity of individuals and societies. For example, human capital refers to the skills, knowledge, and health of people; social capital refers to the networks, trust, and norms that facilitate cooperation and collective action; natural capital refers to the resources and services provided by nature; and cultural capital refers to the values, beliefs, and traditions that shape identity and behavior. Therefore, to measure wealth

35

comprehensively, one needs to account for both tangible and intangible forms of wealth.

How to earn money ethically

One way to earn money ethically is to provide value to others in a way that respects their dignity, autonomy, and rights. This means that one should not exploit, deceive, harm, or coerce others for personal gain. Instead, one should offer goods or services that meet the needs and preferences of others, and that are fair, honest, transparent, and beneficial. For example, one can earn money ethically by creating a product that solves a problem, by teaching a skill that empowers others, by volunteering for a cause that improves society, or by donating to a charity that alleviates suffering. By earning money ethically, one can contribute to the common good and enhance their own well-being.

How to spend money ethically

One way to spend money ethically is to use it in a way that supports the welfare of oneself and others, without causing harm or injustice. This means that one should not waste, hoard, or squander money on things that are unnecessary, harmful, or detrimental. Instead, one should use money wisely and responsibly on things that are essential, beneficial, or meaningful. For example, one can spend money ethically by buying products that are sustainable, ethical, and fair-trade; by supporting businesses that are socially and environmentally responsible; by investing in education, health care, and retirement; or by giving gifts that are thoughtful and personal. By spending money ethically, one can express their values and preferences, and enhance their own happiness and satisfaction.

How to save money ethically

One way to save money ethically is to set aside a portion of one's income for future needs or goals, without depriving oneself or others of current needs or opportunities. This means that one should not save money excessively or obsessively at the expense of living a fulfilling and balanced life. Instead, one should save money moderately and prudently for things that are important or desirable in the long term. For example, one can save money ethically by creating a budget that allocates a reasonable amount for savings; by opening a savings account that offers security and interest; by setting specific and realistic savings goals; or by seeking professional advice on how to optimize their savings strategy. By saving money ethically, one can prepare for contingencies and aspirations, and enhance their own peace of mind and confidence.

36

How to invest money ethically

Investing ethically means choosing companies or funds that align with your values and goals, and that have a positive social and environmental impact. Some examples of ethical investments are renewable energy, green technology, social enterprises, fair trade, human rights, etc. To find ethical investments, you can use online platforms that screen and rate companies or funds based on various criteria, such as ESG (environmental, social and governance) factors, impact investing, sustainable development goals, etc. You can also consult with a financial advisor who specializes in ethical investing or join an ethical investment club or network.

How to donate money ethically

Donating ethically means giving money to charities or causes that are effective, transparent and accountable, and that address the most pressing problems in the world. Some examples of ethical donations are global health, poverty alleviation, animal welfare, climate change, etc. To find ethical donations, you can use online tools that evaluate and compare charities or causes based on various metrics, such as cost-effectiveness, evidence-based interventions, room for more funding, etc. You can also follow the recommendations of experts or organizations that research and promote effective altruism.

How to manage money ethically

Managing money ethically means spending, saving and budgeting money in a way that reflects your values and goals, and that minimizes your negative impact on others and the planet. Some examples of ethical money management are buying less and buying better, saving for the future and emergencies, avoiding debt and interest, supporting local and ethical businesses, etc. To manage money ethically, you can use online tools that help you track your income and expenses, set financial goals and plan your budget. You can also seek advice from a financial coach or counselor who can help you improve your financial literacy and habits.

CHAPTER 10: The Psychology of Wealth

What is the psychology of wealth? It is the study of how our thoughts, emotions, beliefs, and behaviors influence our financial decisions and outcomes. It is also the application of psychological principles and techniques to enhance our wealth creation and management.

The psychology of wealth is important because it can help us understand why we do what we do with money, and how we can change our habits and mindsets to achieve our financial goals. It can also help us overcome the common psychological barriers and biases that prevent us from making optimal choices and taking advantage of opportunities.

In this chapter, we will explore some of the key concepts and topics in the psychology of wealth, such as:

- The difference between a scarcity mindset and an abundance mindset, and how to cultivate the latter
- The role of self-esteem, self-efficacy, and self-worth in wealth creation
- The impact of emotions, such as fear, greed, envy, guilt, and gratitude, on our financial behavior
- The cognitive biases and heuristics that distort our perception and judgment of financial information and situations
- The effects of social influence, such as peer pressure, social comparison, and conformity, on our financial decisions
- The benefits of goal setting, planning, tracking, and feedback for wealth management
- The strategies for developing a positive and healthy relationship with money

38

- The techniques for coping with stress, anxiety, and uncertainty in financial matters

The difference between a scarcity mindset and an abundance mindset, and how to cultivate the latter.

A scarcity mindset is a belief that there is not enough of something, such as money, time, or opportunities, and that one has to compete or hoard resources to survive. An abundance mindset is a belief that there is plenty of everything, and that one can create or attract more resources by being generous, creative, and optimistic. To cultivate an abundance mindset, one can practice gratitude, affirmations, visualization, generosity, and learning.

The role of self-esteem, self-efficacy, and self-worth in wealth creation.

Self-esteem is the evaluation of one's own worthiness and competence. Self-efficacy is the belief in one's ability to achieve goals and overcome challenges. Self-worth is the sense of value and respect that one has for oneself. These three factors are crucial for wealth creation, as they influence one's motivation, confidence, resilience, and decision-making. To improve these factors, one can seek feedback, celebrate successes, challenge negative thoughts, and seek support.

The impact of emotions, such as fear, greed, envy, guilt, and gratitude, on our financial behavior

Emotions are powerful drivers of our actions and reactions, especially in financial matters. Fear can make us avoid risks or sell assets at a loss. Greed can make us chase unrealistic returns or take excessive risks. Envy can make us compare ourselves with others or spend beyond our means. Guilt can make us feel unworthy of wealth or sabotage our success. Gratitude can make us appreciate what we have or share our wealth with others. To manage our emotions effectively, we can identify them, acknowledge them, express them constructively, and learn from them.

The cognitive biases and heuristics that distort our perception and judgment of financial information and situations.

Cognitive biases are systematic errors in thinking that affect our choices and beliefs. Heuristics are mental shortcuts that simplify complex problems or judgments. Some common examples are confirmation bias, anchoring effect, loss aversion, hindsight bias, availability heuristic, and representativeness heuristic. These biases and heuristics can lead us to make irrational or suboptimal financial decisions, such as

39

overestimating our knowledge, ignoring relevant information, avoiding losses at all costs, being influenced by past outcomes, relying on salient or vivid examples, and judging by stereotypes or similarity. To overcome these biases and heuristics, we can seek diverse perspectives, question our assumptions, weigh the pros and cons objectively, review the evidence critically, consider alternative scenarios or explanations, and use analytical tools or methods.

The effects of social influence, such as peer pressure, social comparison, and conformity, on our financial decisions.

Social influence is the change in behavior or attitude that results from the presence or actions of others. Peer pressure is the urge to conform to the expectations or norms of a group or individual. Social comparison is the process of evaluating oneself relative to others. Conformity is the tendency to align one's opinions or behaviors with those of others. These effects can have positive or negative impacts on our financial decisions, depending on the source and direction of the influence. For example, peer pressure can motivate us to save more or spend less, social comparison can inspire us to improve our financial situation or learn from others, and conformity can help us follow best practices or avoid mistakes. However, peer pressure can also tempt us to overspend or overborrow, social comparison can trigger envy or dissatisfaction, and conformity can make us ignore our own preferences or goals. To resist negative social influence, we can assert our individuality, set our own standards, and seek independent advice.

The benefits of goal setting, planning, tracking, and feedback for wealth management.

Goal setting is the process of defining what we want to achieve and how we will measure our progress. Planning is the process of devising a course of action to reach our goals. Tracking is the process of monitoring our performance and results. Feedback is the process of receiving information or evaluation on our actions or outcomes. These four steps are essential for wealth management, as they help us clarify our vision, focus our efforts, adjust our strategies, and improve our skills. To apply these steps effectively, we can use SMART criteria (Specific, Measurable, Achievable, Relevant, and Time-bound) for goal setting, use budgeting tools or apps for planning, use spreadsheets or statements for tracking, and use mentors or coaches for feedback.

The strategies for developing a positive and healthy relationship with money.

A positive and healthy relationship with money is one that is based on respect,

40

responsibility, and reality. Respect means treating money as a valuable resource that deserves care and appreciation. Responsibility means managing money wisely and ethically, according to our needs and values. Reality means accepting money as a tool and a means, not an end or a source of happiness. To develop such a relationship with money, we can adopt some strategies, such as recognizing our money beliefs and patterns, aligning our money behavior with our life purpose, balancing our spending and saving habits, embracing abundance and generosity, and seeking financial education and guidance.

The techniques for coping with stress, anxiety, and uncertainty in financial matters.

Stress, anxiety, and uncertainty are common emotions that arise in financial matters, especially in times of crisis or change. They can affect our physical and mental health,
as well as our financial performance and well-being. To cope with these emotions effectively, we can use some techniques, such as breathing exercises, meditation, or yoga for relaxation, positive affirmations, visualization, or journaling for empowerment, problem-solving, action-planning, or contingency-planning for control, social support, counseling, or therapy for relief, and humor, hobbies, or hobbies for enjoyment.

By learning and applying the psychology of wealth, we can improve our financial literacy, intelligence, and well-being. We can also increase our chances of achieving financial freedom and fulfillment.

CHAPTER 11: The Relationships of Wealth

One of the most important aspects of wealth creation is the relationships you have with other people. Your relationships can either support or hinder your wealth journey, depending on how you manage them. In this chapter, we will explore the different types of relationships that affect your wealth, and how to cultivate them for your benefit.

The first type of relationship is with yourself. This is the foundation of all other relationships, and the most crucial one. How you see yourself, how you value yourself, and how you treat yourself will determine how others see, value, and treat you. If you have a positive self-image, a high self-esteem, and a healthy self-care routine, you will attract people who respect you, appreciate you, and want to help you. If you have a negative self-image, a low self-esteem, and a poor self-care routine, you will attract people who disrespect you, take advantage of you, and want to harm you.

The second type of relationship is with your family. This includes your parents, siblings, spouse, children, and other relatives. Your family can be a source of love, support, guidance, and inspiration for your wealth creation. They can also be a source of stress, conflict, criticism, and distraction. The key is to balance your family obligations with your personal goals, and to communicate clearly and respectfully with your family members. You should also set healthy boundaries with your family, and avoid letting them interfere with your financial decisions.

The third type of relationship is with your friends. This includes your peers, colleagues, mentors, partners, and associates. Your friends can be a source of fun, joy, learning, collaboration, and feedback for your wealth creation. They can also be a source of envy, jealousy, competition, sabotage, and negativity. The key is to choose your friends wisely, and to surround yourself with people who share your vision, values, and interests. You should also be a good friend to others, and offer them support, encouragement, and advice when needed.

The fourth type of relationship is with your customers. This includes your clients, prospects, fans, followers, and subscribers. Your customers are the lifeblood of your business, and the reason why you create value in the market. Your customers can be a source of income, loyalty,

42

referrals, testimonials, and feedback for your wealth creation. They can also be a source of complaints, refunds, disputes, bad reviews, and lawsuits. The key is to serve your customers well, and to exceed their expectations. You should also listen to your customers' needs and wants, and adapt your products or services accordingly.

The fifth type of relationship is with your competitors. This includes your rivals, opponents, challengers, and adversaries. Your competitors are the ones who offer similar or alternative products or services to yours in the market. Your competitors can be a source of motivation, innovation, improvement, and differentiation for your wealth creation. They can also be a source of frustration, stress, conflict, and loss. The key is to respect your competitors, and to learn from them. You should also differentiate yourself from your competitors, and offer something unique or better to your customers.

These are the five types of relationships that affect your wealth creation. By cultivating positive and productive relationships with yourself, your family, your friends, your customers, and your competitors, you will enhance your chances of achieving wealth and success. Remember that wealth is not only about money, but also about happiness, fulfillment, and contribution. And these are all influenced by the quality of your relationships.

CHAPTER 12: The Lifestyle of Wealth

What does it mean to live a wealthy lifestyle? Is it about having expensive cars, clothes, and houses? Is it about traveling the world, eating at fancy restaurants, and staying at luxury hotels? Is it about being able to do whatever you want, whenever you want, with whoever you want?

The answer is: it depends.

Wealth is not a one-size-fits-all concept. It is a subjective and personal experience that varies from person to person. What makes one person happy and fulfilled may not be the same for another. Therefore, there is no single definition or formula for a wealthy lifestyle. Rather, there are principles and guidelines that can help you create your own version of a wealthy lifestyle that suits your values, goals, and preferences.

In this chapter, we will explore some of these principles and guidelines, and how they can help you design and enjoy a lifestyle that reflects your true wealth.

Principle 1: Align your lifestyle with your purpose

One of the most important aspects of a wealthy lifestyle is alignment. Alignment means that your lifestyle is congruent with your purpose, or your reason for being. Your purpose is what gives meaning and direction to your life. It is what motivates you to get up in the morning and pursue your dreams. It is what makes you feel alive and fulfilled.

When your lifestyle is aligned with your purpose, you are living authentically and intentionally. You are not wasting your time, energy, or money on things that do not matter to you or contribute to your happiness. You are not living by someone else's standards or expectations. You are living by your own.

44

To align your lifestyle with your purpose, you need to first discover your purpose. This may not be an easy or quick process, but it is worth the effort. You can start by asking yourself some questions, such as:

- What are you passionate about?
- What are you good at?
- What do you enjoy doing?
- What are the problems or needs that you want to solve or address?
- What are the values that guide your decisions and actions?
- What are the goals that you want to achieve in your life?
- What are the roles that you play in your life (e.g., parent, spouse, friend, etc.)?
- What are the legacy that you want to leave behind?

By answering these questions, you can gain more clarity and insight into your purpose. You can then use this as a compass to guide your lifestyle choices. For example, if your purpose is to help others improve their health and well-being, you may choose a lifestyle that involves working as a health coach, volunteering at a local clinic, joining a fitness club, eating nutritious food, meditating regularly, etc. These choices will not only support your purpose, but also make you feel happy and fulfilled.

Principle 2: Balance your lifestyle with your needs

Another important aspect of a wealthy lifestyle is balance. Balance means that your lifestyle meets your needs in different areas of your life, such as physical, mental, emotional, social, spiritual, etc. Your needs are what keep you healthy and well-functioning. They are what sustain and nourish you.

When your lifestyle is balanced with your needs, you are living harmoniously and holistically. You are not neglecting or sacrificing any aspect of your well-being for another. You are not overdoing or underdoing anything. You are doing just enough to maintain and enhance your well-being.

To balance your lifestyle with your needs, you need to first identify your needs in different areas of your life. You can use a tool such as the Wheel of Life to assess how satisfied you are with each area of your life on a scale of 1 to 10. The areas may include:

45

- Health
- Career
- Finances
- Relationships
- Personal Growth
- Fun and Recreation
- Environment
- Spirituality

By doing this exercise, you can see which areas of your life need more attention or improvement. You can then use this as a basis to adjust your lifestyle accordingly. For example, if you score low on health, you may choose a lifestyle that involves exercising more often, sleeping better, drinking more water, etc. If you score low on fun and recreation, you may choose a lifestyle that involves taking more breaks, pursuing hobbies, traveling more often, etc.

Principle 3: Optimize your lifestyle with your resources

A third important aspect of a wealthy lifestyle is optimization. Optimization means that you make the best use of what you have, whether it is money, time, energy, skills, or relationships. Optimization helps you achieve your goals faster and more efficiently, while avoiding waste and unnecessary expenses. Here are some examples of how to optimize your lifestyle with your resources:

- **Money:** You can optimize your money by creating a budget, tracking your expenses, saving and investing wisely, and spending on things that bring you value and happiness. You can also optimize your money by reducing your debt, avoiding fees and interest charges, and taking advantage of discounts and rewards programs.

- **Time:** You can optimize your time by prioritizing your tasks, setting deadlines, delegating or outsourcing what you can, and eliminating distractions and procrastination. You can also optimize your time by scheduling your activities according to your energy levels, using tools and apps that automate or simplify your work, and creating routines and habits that make you more productive.

- **Energy:** You can optimize your energy by taking care of your physical and mental health, eating well, sleeping enough, exercising regularly, and

46

managing your stress. You can also optimize your energy by finding your passion, doing what you love, learning new things, and having fun.

- **Skills:** You can optimize your skills by identifying your strengths and weaknesses, setting learning goals, seeking feedback and mentorship, and practicing deliberately. You can also optimize your skills by applying them to real-world problems, teaching others what you know, and challenging yourself to improve.

- **Relationships:** You can optimize your relationships by choosing the right people to surround yourself with, communicating effectively, expressing gratitude and appreciation, and supporting and helping others. You can also optimize your relationships by resolving conflicts peacefully, respecting boundaries and differences, and nurturing trust and intimacy.

47

CHAPTER 13: The Legacy of Wealth

What will you leave behind when you are gone? How will you be remembered by your family, friends, community, and the world? How will your wealth impact the lives of others, both now and in the future? These are some of the questions that you need to ask yourself if you want to create a lasting legacy of wealth.

A legacy of wealth is not just about money. It is about the values, principles, and lessons that you pass on to the next generation. It is about the causes, missions, and visions that you support and advance with your wealth. It is about the impact that you make on the world with your wealth.

Creating a legacy of wealth requires intention, planning, and action. You need to have a clear vision of what you want your legacy to be, and how you want to achieve it. You need to have a plan for how you will distribute your wealth, both during your lifetime and after your death. You need to take action to implement your plan, and to communicate it with your loved ones and advisors.

There are many ways to create a legacy of wealth, depending on your goals, values, and preferences. Some of the common methods include:

- Creating a will or a trust that specifies how you want your assets to be distributed among your heirs and beneficiaries.
- Establishing a family foundation or a donor-advised fund that supports charitable causes that align with your values and passions.
- Setting up a scholarship or an endowment that provides educational opportunities for students or researchers in your field of interest.
- Writing a book or a memoir that shares your life story, insights, and wisdom with the world.

48

- Mentoring or coaching others who aspire to follow in your footsteps or learn from your experience.
- Creating a product or a service that solves a problem or improves the quality of life for others.
- Developing a system or a model that innovates or transforms an industry or a sector.
- Launching a movement or a campaign that advocates for a social or environmental change.

Whatever method you choose, remember that creating a legacy of wealth is not a one-time event. It is an ongoing process that requires constant review, evaluation, and adjustment. You need to monitor the performance and impact of your legacy activities, and make changes as needed. You also need to update your plan as your circumstances, goals, and values change over time.

Creating a legacy of wealth is one of the most rewarding and fulfilling aspects of wealth creation. It allows you to extend your influence beyond your lifetime, and to make a positive difference in the world. It also gives you a sense of purpose, meaning, and satisfaction in life. By creating a legacy of wealth, you are not only enriching yourself, but also enriching others.

CHAPTER 14: The Future of Wealth

What will wealth look like in the future? How will the world change as more people become wealthy? How can you prepare for the challenges and opportunities that lie ahead? These are some of the questions that this chapter will explore.

The future of wealth is not a fixed or predetermined outcome. It is a dynamic and evolving process that depends on many factors, such as technology, innovation, globalization, demographics, environment, politics, culture, and ethics. However, some trends and patterns can be observed and projected based on the current state of affairs and the historical evidence.

One of the most obvious and significant trends is the increasing democratization of wealth. Thanks to the internet, education, entrepreneurship, and financial inclusion, more people have access to the resources and opportunities to create, manage, and multiply their money. According to the Credit Suisse Global Wealth Report 2021, there were 56.1 million millionaires in the world in 2020, up from 42.2 million in 2019. The report also estimates that by 2025, there will be 84 million millionaires and 1.7 billion adults with wealth above $10,000.

Another trend is the diversification of wealth. Wealth is no longer concentrated in a few regions or countries. It is spreading across the globe, especially in emerging markets like China, India, Brazil, Russia, and Indonesia. These countries are experiencing rapid economic growth, social development, and political influence. They are also producing new wealthy individuals and families who have different values, preferences, and behaviors than their counterparts in developed countries.

A third trend is the digitalization of wealth. Technology is transforming every aspect of wealth creation, management, and multiplication. From online platforms, apps, and tools that enable people to save, invest, trade, borrow, lend, donate, and spend their money more efficiently and effectively; to artificial intelligence, blockchain, biotechnology, nanotechnology, and quantum computing that offer new possibilities and challenges for wealth generation and preservation; to virtual reality, augmented reality, metaverse, and gamification that create new experiences and opportunities for wealth enjoyment and expression.

50

These trends have profound implications for the future of wealth. They also pose new questions and dilemmas for wealthy individuals and society as a whole. For instance:

- How will wealth inequality affect social cohesion, political stability, and human dignity?
- How will wealth mobility affect cultural diversity, national identity, and global citizenship?
- How will wealth security affect personal privacy, data protection, and cyber resilience?
- How will wealth responsibility affect environmental sustainability, social justice, and ethical standards?
- How will wealth meaning affect personal fulfillment, happiness, and well-being?

These are not easy questions to answer. They require a holistic and multidimensional approach that considers not only the financial aspects of wealth but also its psychological, emotional, social, spiritual, and moral dimensions. They also require a long-term and visionary perspective that anticipates the changes and challenges that lie ahead.

You have a unique opportunity to explore these questions and share your insights with people. You can also use your skills and talents to inspire, educate, and empower them to create, manage, and multiply their money in a way that aligns with their values, goals, and purpose.

CHAPTER 15: The Secrets of Wealth

You have learned a lot about wealth in this book. You have learned what wealth is, why it matters, how to create it, how to manage it, how to multiply it, and how to enjoy it. You have learned the pillars, the mindset, the habits, the skills, the strategies, the tools, the risks, the ethics, the psychology, the relationships, the lifestyle, and the legacy of wealth. You have learned how wealth can help you achieve your goals, fulfill your purpose, and make a positive impact in the world.

But there is something else you need to know about wealth. Something that most people don't know. Something that most books don't tell you. Something that can make a huge difference in your wealth journey. Something that can give you an edge over others. Something that can unlock new levels of wealth for you.

These are the secrets of wealth.

What are the secrets of wealth? They are not magic formulas or hidden codes. They are not illegal schemes or unethical shortcuts. They are not mystical secrets or esoteric knowledge. They are simply principles, insights, and practices that are not widely known or understood by most people. They are secrets because they are either ignored, overlooked, or underestimated by most people.

But they are not secrets for you anymore. In this chapter, you will discover some of the most powerful secrets of wealth that can transform your financial life. You will learn how to apply them to your own situation and benefit from them. You will learn how to use them to create more wealth, faster and easier than ever before.

Here are some of the secrets of wealth that you will learn in this chapter:

52

- How to leverage the power of compounding to grow your wealth exponentially
- How to use the 80/20 rule to focus on the most important and profitable activities
- How to create multiple streams of income to diversify and increase your cash flow
- How to use debt wisely and strategically to accelerate your wealth creation
- How to invest in yourself and your education to increase your value and income
- How to leverage other people's time, money, skills, and resources to multiply your results
- How to master the art of negotiation and persuasion to get better deals and opportunities
- How to build a strong personal brand and network to attract more customers and partners
- How to use systems and automation to simplify and scale your business and income
- How to tap into your passion and purpose to create wealth that is meaningful and fulfilling

These are just some of the secrets of wealth that you will learn in this chapter. There are many more secrets that you can discover and apply in your own journey. The more secrets you know and use, the more wealth you can create and enjoy.

But remember: knowing these secrets is not enough. You have to act on them. You have to implement them in your daily life. You have to make them part of your habits and routines. You have to test them, tweak them, and improve them. You have to master them.

Only then will you be able to unlock the full potential of these secrets of wealth.

Are you ready to learn these secrets? Are you ready to apply them? Are you ready to transform your financial life?

If yes, then let's begin.

How to leverage the power of compounding to grow your wealth exponentially

One of the most powerful concepts in personal finance is the power of compounding. Compounding means that your money grows faster over time as you earn interest on both your principal and your accumulated interest. For example, if you invest $10,000 at a 10% annual interest rate, you will have $11,000 after one year. But if you reinvest the interest, you will have $12,100 after two years, $13,310 after three years, and so on. After 10 years, you will have $25,937, more than doubling your initial investment. The longer you let your money compound, the faster it grows exponentially.

How to use the 80/20 rule to focus on the most important and profitable activities

Another key concept in personal finance is the 80/20 rule, also known as the Pareto principle. This rule states that 80% of the results come from 20% of the causes. For example, 80% of your income may come from 20% of your clients, or 80% of your expenses may come from 20% of your purchases. The 80/20 rule can help you focus on the most important and profitable activities and eliminate or reduce the ones that are not. For example, you can identify and prioritize the 20% of your tasks that generate 80% of your value, or the 20% of your habits that improve 80% of your health.

How to create multiple streams of income to diversify and increase your cash flow

A third concept that can help you improve your personal finance is creating multiple streams of income. Having multiple streams of income means that you have more than one source of money coming in every month. This can help you diversify and increase your cash flow, as well as protect you from losing your income if one stream dries up. For example, you can create multiple streams of income by having a salary, a side hustle, a rental property, dividends from stocks, royalties from books or music, etc. The more streams of income you have, the more financial security and freedom you can enjoy.

How to use debt wisely and strategically to accelerate your wealth creation

Debt is often seen as a negative thing, but it can also be a powerful tool for wealth creation if used wisely and strategically. Debt allows you to access more capital than you have, and use it to invest in assets that generate income or appreciate in value over time. For example, you can use debt to buy a rental property, a business, or a stock portfolio, and earn passive income from them. However, not all debt is created equal. You should only use debt for productive purposes, and avoid consumer debt

54

that does not generate any return, such as credit cards, car loans, or personal loans. You should also compare the interest rate of the debt with the expected return of the investment, and make sure you can afford the monthly payments and have a plan to pay off the debt eventually.

How to invest in yourself and your education to increase your value and income

Another way to accelerate your wealth creation is to invest in yourself and your education. You are your most valuable asset, and your skills, knowledge, and experience determine your earning potential. By investing in yourself, you can increase your value and income in the market, and open up more opportunities for growth and advancement. For example, you can invest in yourself by taking courses, reading books, attending seminars, getting certifications, or hiring a coach or mentor. You can also invest in your education by pursuing a degree, a diploma, or a certificate that can boost your credentials and qualifications. However, you should also be careful not to overinvest in education that does not have a clear return on investment, or that does not align with your goals and passions.

How to leverage other people's time, money, skills, and resources to multiply your results

You can leverage other people's time, money, skills, and resources to multiply your results. You do not have to do everything by yourself, or rely on your own limited resources. You can leverage other people's time by outsourcing tasks that are not your core competencies, or that do not add value to your business or life. For example, you can hire a virtual assistant, a freelancer, or a contractor to handle administrative work, marketing, accounting, or other functions that you are not good at or enjoy doing. You can leverage other people's money by raising capital from investors, partners, lenders, or crowdfunding platforms to fund your projects or ventures. For example, you can pitch your idea to angel investors, venture capitalists, banks, or online platforms to get the funding you need to start or grow your business. You can leverage other people's skills by collaborating with experts, mentors, coaches, consultants, or advisors who can provide you with guidance, feedback, advice, or support. For example, you can join a mastermind group, a networking group, or a mentoring program to learn from others who have achieved what you want to achieve. You can leverage other people's resources by using tools, platforms, systems, or networks that can enhance your productivity, efficiency, or reach. For example, you can use software, apps, websites, or social media to automate tasks, manage projects, communicate with customers, or market your products or services.

55

How to master the art of negotiation and persuasion to get better deals and opportunities

Negotiation and persuasion are essential skills for any entrepreneur who wants to succeed in the competitive and dynamic market. Negotiation is the process of reaching an agreement with another party that benefits both sides, while persuasion is the art of influencing someone's attitude, beliefs or actions. To master these skills, you need to understand the psychology of human behavior, the principles of effective communication, and the strategies of win-win scenarios. Some tips to improve your negotiation and persuasion skills are:

- **Prepare well before any negotiation or persuasion attempt.** Research the other party's needs, interests, goals, strengths and weaknesses. Anticipate their objections and concerns, and plan how to address them. Also, set your own objectives and limits, and know what you are willing to compromise on and what you are not.

- **Build rapport and trust with the other party.** Use positive body language, eye contact, and active listening to show respect and empathy. Find common ground and shared values, and emphasize them throughout the conversation. Avoid confrontational or aggressive language, and focus on the benefits of cooperation rather than competition.

- **Use logic and emotion to persuade the other party.** Provide facts, data, and evidence to support your arguments, but also appeal to their emotions and desires. Use stories, anecdotes, and testimonials to illustrate your points and make them more memorable. Use positive framing and language to highlight the advantages of your proposal, and contrast them with the drawbacks of the alternatives.

- **Be flexible and creative in finding solutions.** Don't get stuck on your initial position or demand, but be open to explore different options and alternatives. Look for ways to create value for both sides, and avoid zero-sum thinking. Seek win-win outcomes that satisfy both parties' interests and needs, and avoid win-lose or lose-lose situations that damage the relationship.

How to build a strong personal brand and network to attract more customers and partners

56

Personal branding and networking are powerful tools for any entrepreneur who wants to stand out from the crowd and attract more opportunities. Personal branding is the process of creating a unique identity and reputation for yourself, based on your values, strengths, skills, and passions. Networking is the process of building and maintaining relationships with people who can help you achieve your goals, such as customers, partners, mentors, peers, or influencers. To build a strong personal brand and network, you need to:

- **Define your niche and target audience.** Identify what makes you different and valuable in your field, and who are the people who need or want what you offer. Focus on a specific problem or solution that you can provide better than anyone else, and communicate it clearly and consistently.

- **Create and share valuable content.** Establish yourself as an authority and a thought leader in your niche by creating and sharing content that showcases your expertise, insights, opinions, and personality. Use different platforms and formats, such as blogs, podcasts, videos, social media posts, newsletters, e-books, webinars, etc., to reach your audience and engage them.

- **Connect and collaborate with others.** Expand your network by reaching out to people who share your interests, values, or goals. Attend events, join communities, participate in discussions, offer help or advice, ask for feedback or referrals, etc. Also, look for opportunities to collaborate with others on projects or initiatives that can benefit both parties.

- **Be authentic and consistent.** The most important aspect of personal branding and networking is authenticity. Be yourself, be honest, be transparent. Don't try to be someone you are not or pretend to know something you don't. Don't make promises you can't keep or exaggerate your achievements or results. Be consistent in your message, style, and actions across all platforms and interactions.

How to use systems and automation to simplify and scale your business and income

Systems and automation are essential for any entrepreneur who wants to simplify and scale their business and income. Systems are the processes and procedures that run your business efficiently and effectively. Automation is the use of technology or

57

tools to perform tasks that would otherwise require human intervention or effort. To use systems and automation to grow your business and income, you need to:

- **Identify and document your core processes.** Analyze your business operations and identify the key activities that generate value for your customers or clients. These could be product development, marketing, sales, delivery, support, etc. Document each process step by step, and define the roles, responsibilities, and resources involved.

- **Optimize and streamline your processes.** Look for ways to improve your processes by eliminating waste, reducing errors, increasing quality, or enhancing customer satisfaction. Use tools such as flowcharts, diagrams, checklists, templates, etc., to simplify and standardize your processes.

- **Automate and delegate your tasks.** Identify the tasks that are repetitive, routine, or low-value in your processes, and automate them using technology or tools. These could be software, apps, bots, scripts, etc., that can perform functions such as scheduling, invoicing, emailing, reporting, etc. Also, identify the tasks that are high-value but not your core competency, and delegate them to someone else who can do them better or faster. These could be freelancers, contractors, employees, partners, etc., who can handle tasks such as design, writing, accounting, legal, etc.

- **Monitor and measure your results.** Track and analyze the performance and outcomes of your processes and tasks, and use data and feedback to evaluate their effectiveness and efficiency. Use metrics and indicators such as revenue, profit, cost, time, quality, customer satisfaction, etc., to measure your results. Also, use tools such as dashboards, charts, graphs, etc., to visualize and communicate your results.

How to tap into your passion and purpose to create wealth that is meaningful and fulfilling

Passion and purpose are the driving forces behind any successful entrepreneur who wants to create wealth that is meaningful and fulfilling. Passion is the intense enthusiasm and interest that you have for something that you love or enjoy. Purpose is the clear and compelling vision that you have for the impact that you want to make in the world or the value that you want to create for others. To tap into your passion and purpose to create wealth, you need to:

58

- **Discover your passion and purpose.** Explore your interests, hobbies, talents, skills, values, and dreams, and find out what makes you happy, excited, and fulfilled. Ask yourself questions such as: What do I love to do? What am I good at? What do I care about? What do I want to achieve? What problems do I want to solve? What difference do I want to make?

- **Align your passion and purpose with your business.** Find a way to turn your passion and purpose into a profitable business model that can generate income and value for yourself and others. Look for a market need or opportunity that matches your passion and purpose, and create a product or service that can satisfy it. Validate your idea by testing it with potential customers or clients, and get feedback and support from mentors, peers, or experts.

- **Pursue your passion and purpose with persistence and resilience.** Pursuing your passion and purpose is not easy, and you will face many challenges, obstacles, and setbacks along the way. To overcome them, you need to have a strong mindset and attitude that can keep you motivated, focused, and optimistic. Set realistic and specific goals, and break them down into manageable steps. Celebrate your achievements and learn from your failures. Seek help when you need it, and surround yourself with positive and supportive people.

- **Share your passion and purpose with others.** The ultimate goal of creating wealth from your passion and purpose is to share it with others who can benefit from it or appreciate it. Use your wealth to make a positive difference in the world or in the lives of others, whether it is by creating jobs, supporting causes, donating to charities, mentoring others, etc. Also, inspire others to follow their own passion and purpose by sharing your story, insights, lessons, or advice.

CHAPTER 16: The Myths of Wealth

Wealth is a topic that attracts a lot of attention, curiosity and fascination. However, it also generates a lot of confusion, misunderstanding and misconception. There are many myths about wealth that prevent people from achieving their financial goals and living their desired lifestyle. In this chapter, we will debunk some of the most common and harmful myths of wealth and reveal the truth behind them.

Myth #1: Wealth is only for the lucky, the smart or the privileged.

This myth implies that wealth is a matter of chance, intelligence or birthright. It suggests that wealth is something that you either have or don't have, and that you can't do much to change it. This is a very limiting and disempowering belief that keeps people stuck in a scarcity mindset.

The truth is that wealth is for anyone who is willing to learn, work and grow. Wealth is not a fixed or finite resource that only a few can access. Wealth is a dynamic and abundant phenomenon that can be created, managed and multiplied by anyone who follows the principles and practices of wealth creation. Wealth is not a lottery, a test or a privilege. Wealth is a skill, a strategy and a choice.

Myth #2: Wealth is measured by how much money you have.

This myth equates wealth with money and assumes that the more money you have, the wealthier you are. It focuses on the quantity of money rather than the quality of money. It ignores the fact that money is only one aspect of wealth and that there are other dimensions of wealth that are equally or more important.

60

The truth is that wealth is measured by how much value you create, how much impact you make and how much freedom you enjoy. Wealth is not just about having money, but about using money as a tool to achieve your purpose, to serve your values and to fulfill your vision. Wealth is not just about accumulating money, but about allocating money in alignment with your goals, your passions and your priorities. Wealth is not just about counting money, but about living money.

Myth #3: Wealth is the source of happiness.

This myth assumes that wealth can buy happiness and that the more wealth you have, the happier you will be. It creates a false expectation that wealth will solve all your problems, fulfill all your needs and satisfy all your desires. It leads to an endless pursuit of more wealth without ever feeling enough or content.

The truth is that wealth is not the source of happiness, but the result of happiness. Happiness comes from within, not from without. Happiness is a state of mind, not a state of affairs. Happiness is based on who you are, not on what you have. Happiness is not dependent on wealth, but on how you relate to wealth. Happiness is not determined by wealth, but by how you use wealth to enhance your well-being and the well-being of others.

CHAPTER 17: The Opportunities of Wealth

One of the most important aspects of wealth creation is the ability to recognize and seize the opportunities that are available to you. Opportunities are everywhere, but not everyone can see them or act on them. Opportunities are the openings that allow you to create value, to solve problems, to serve others, to make a difference, to grow, to learn, to contribute, to enjoy, to fulfill your potential. Opportunities are the fuel that drives your wealth engine.

But how do you find and exploit the opportunities of wealth? How do you turn your ideas into reality? How do you overcome the obstacles and challenges that inevitably arise? How do you manage the risks and uncertainties that come with any venture? How do you leverage your resources and network to maximize your impact? How do you balance your passion and purpose with your profit and performance?

In this chapter, we will explore the answers to these questions and more. We will share with you the principles and practices that successful wealth creators use to identify, evaluate, pursue and execute the opportunities of wealth. We will show you how to develop an opportunity mindset, how to cultivate an opportunity environment, how to apply an opportunity framework and how to implement an opportunity system. We will also give you some examples and case studies of people who have used these methods to create extraordinary wealth in various fields and industries.

Let's start with the opportunity mindset. The opportunity mindset is the way of thinking that enables you to see the possibilities and potentials in any situation. It is the attitude that makes you curious, creative, optimistic, resilient and proactive. It is the mindset that helps you overcome fear, doubt, inertia and complacency. It is the mindset that motivates you to take action and make things happen.

The opportunity mindset is based on four key beliefs:

62

1) **There is always a way.** No matter how difficult or complex the problem is, there is always a solution. No matter how competitive or crowded the market is, there is always a niche. No matter how scarce or limited the resources are, there is always a way to use them efficiently and effectively.

2) **There is always a need.** No matter how satisfied or happy the customers are, there is always a way to serve them better. No matter how advanced or sophisticated the technology is, there is always a way to improve it. No matter how abundant or diverse the information is, there is always a way to organize it and make it accessible.

3) **There is always a value.** No matter how common or ordinary the product or service is, there is always a way to make it unique and desirable. No matter how low or high the price is, there is always a way to make it fair and profitable. No matter how simple or complex the process is, there is always a way to make it efficient and effective.

4) **There is always a learning.** No matter how successful or unsuccessful the outcome is, there is always a way to learn from it. No matter how familiar or unfamiliar the situation is, there is always a way to gain new insights and perspectives. No matter how easy or hard the challenge is, there is always a way to grow and improve.

These beliefs are not naive or unrealistic. They are based on evidence and experience. They are based on the stories of countless entrepreneurs, innovators, leaders and achievers who have used them to create wealth in different domains and contexts.

For example, consider the story of Sara Blakely, the founder of Spanx, a company that sells shapewear for women. Sara was working as a salesperson for an office supply company when she had an idea for a product that would smooth out panty lines under white pants. She cut off the feet of her pantyhose and wore them under her pants. She liked the result, but she realized that there was no product like that in the market. She decided to create her own.

She faced many obstacles along the way. She had no experience in fashion or manufacturing. She had no money or connections. She had no patent or trademark protection. She had no distribution or marketing channels. She had no business plan or strategy.

63

But she had an opportunity mindset. She believed that there was a way, a need, a value and a learning in her idea. She researched the industry and found a manufacturer who agreed to make her product. She invested her savings of $5,000 into her business. She applied for a patent by herself using a textbook from Barnes & Noble. She created her own logo and packaging using Microsoft Word. She persuaded Neiman Marcus to carry her product by demonstrating it in their bathroom. She generated publicity by sending samples to Oprah Winfrey's show.

She did all this while keeping her day job as a salesperson until she was able to quit and focus on her business full-time.

Today, Spanx is a global brand with over $400 million in annual revenue and over 200 products for women and men.

Sara Blakely's story is just one of many examples of how the opportunity mindset can help you create wealth. You can find more examples in the books, podcasts, blogs and videos of authors, speakers, coaches and mentors who specialize in this topic.

The opportunity mindset is not something you are born with. It is something you can develop and cultivate. You can do this by exposing yourself to inspiring and empowering stories, by surrounding yourself with positive and supportive people, by challenging yourself with new and exciting experiences, by reflecting on your successes and failures, by asking yourself empowering questions, by setting yourself clear and realistic goals, by taking action and making progress, by celebrating your achievements and learning from your mistakes.

The opportunity mindset is the foundation of wealth creation. Without it, you will miss or ignore the opportunities that are around you. With it, you will see and seize the opportunities that are waiting for you.

But having an opportunity mindset is not enough. You also need to have an opportunity environment. The opportunity environment is the external context that enables you to pursue and execute the opportunities that you find. It is the physical, social, cultural, economic and political factors that influence your wealth creation process.

The opportunity environment is based on four key elements:

1) **Resources.** Resources are the assets that you have or can access to create value. They include money, time, energy, skills, knowledge, tools, equipment, materials, information, data, etc.

2) **Network.** Network is the people that you know or can connect with to create value. They include customers, suppliers, partners, investors, mentors, advisors, peers, friends, family, etc.

3) **Market.** Market is the place where you can exchange value with others. It includes the industry, sector, niche, segment, category, platform, channel, etc.

4) **System.** System is the rules and regulations that govern your value creation process. It includes the laws, policies, standards, norms, ethics, culture, etc.

These elements are not fixed or static. They are dynamic and changing. They are affected by trends and events that happen locally and globally. They are influenced by forces and factors that are beyond your control.

For example,

- Resources can increase or decrease depending on your income and expenses
- Network can expand or contract depending on your relationships and interactions
- Market can grow or shrink depending on the demand and supply
- System can enable or disable depending on the incentives and constraints

These elements are not independent or isolated. They are interdependent and interconnected. They affect each other in positive and negative ways.

For example,

- Resources can help you build your network by investing in your relationships
- Network can help you access more resources by sharing information and referrals
- Market can help you leverage your resources by creating demand for your products or services
- System can help you protect your market by providing legal and ethical frameworks

65

These elements are not equal or balanced. They are relative and variable. They have different levels of importance and influence depending on your situation and goals.

For example,

- Resources may be more important than network if you have a capital-intensive business
- Network may be more important than resources if you have a service-based business
- Market may be more important than system if you have a disruptive innovation
- System may be more important than market if you have a regulated industry

The opportunity environment is not something you take for granted. It is something you analyze and optimize. You can do this by assessing the strengths and weaknesses of each element in relation to your opportunity. You can do this by identifying the opportunities and threats that each element presents to your opportunity. You can do this by aligning your opportunity with the elements that support it and avoiding or overcoming the elements that hinder it.

The opportunity environment is the context of wealth creation. Without it, you will face difficulties or dangers in pursuing and executing your opportunities. With it, you will have advantages or benefits in pursuing and executing your opportunities.

But having an opportunity environment is not enough. You also need to have an opportunity framework. The opportunity framework is the way of organizing and evaluating your opportunities based on their potential value and feasibility. It is the method that helps you decide which opportunities to pursue and which ones to ignore or postpone.

The opportunity framework is based on four key criteria:

1) **Problem.** Problem is the pain or gap that your opportunity addresses for your target customer or beneficiary.

2) **Solution.** Solution is the product or service that your opportunity provides to solve the problem or fill the gap.

3) **Model.** Model is the way that your opportunity generates revenue or impact from delivering the solution to the problem.

4) **Edge.** Edge is the advantage or differentiation that your opportunity has over other alternatives or competitors.

These criteria are not absolute or objective. They are relative and subjective. They depend on how you define them and how others perceive them. For example, a problem that is urgent and important for one customer segment may be irrelevant or trivial for another. A solution that is innovative and effective for one market may be outdated and inefficient for another. A model that is profitable and scalable for one industry may be unfeasible and unsustainable for another. An edge that is unique and compelling for one stakeholder may be common and insignificant for another.

Therefore, it is important to use the opportunity framework as a guide, not a formula. It can help you clarify and refine your opportunity, but it cannot guarantee its success. You still need to test and validate your assumptions, gather feedback from your customers and partners, and adapt to changing conditions and circumstances.

CHAPTER 18: The Wisdom of Wealth

In the previous chapters, we have explored the various aspects of wealth creation, management and multiplication. We have learned about the concept, the pillars, the mindset, the habits, the skills, the strategies, the tools, the risks, the ethics, the psychology, the relationships, the lifestyle, the legacy, the future, the secrets, the myths and the opportunities of wealth. But what is the ultimate purpose of wealth? What is the meaning of wealth? How can we use wealth to enrich our lives and the lives of others? How can we achieve not only financial success, but also personal fulfillment and happiness? These are some of the questions that we will address in this chapter, which is about the wisdom of wealth.

The wisdom of wealth is not about how much money you have, but how you use it. It is not about how smart you are, but how you apply your knowledge. It is not about how hard you work, but how you balance your work and your life. It is not about how many goals you achieve, but how you enjoy the journey. It is not about how many people you impress, but how you impact them. It is not about how much you own, but how much you give. The wisdom of wealth is about finding your true purpose, your passion, your values and your vision. It is about aligning your actions with your intentions. It is about living authentically, creatively and generously. It is about making a positive difference in the world.

The wisdom of wealth is not something that you can learn from a book or a course. It is something that you can only discover through your own experience and reflection. It is something that you can only develop through your own trials and errors, successes and failures, joys and sorrows. It is something that you can only cultivate through your own curiosity and openness, humility and gratitude, courage and resilience. The wisdom of wealth is not a destination that you can reach, but a journey that you can embark on. It is not a fixed state that you can attain, but a

68

dynamic process that you can engage in. It is not a final answer that you can find, but a lifelong quest that you can pursue.

The wisdom of wealth is not a one-size-fits-all formula that you can apply to everyone and every situation. It is a personal and contextual expression that you can adapt to your own circumstances and preferences. It is a flexible and evolving framework that you can modify to your own challenges and opportunities. It is a creative and experimental approach that you can customize to your own goals and dreams. The wisdom of wealth is not a rigid set of rules that you have to follow, but a set of principles that you can choose to adopt. It is not a dogmatic doctrine that you have to believe in, but a set of insights that you can explore and test.

The wisdom of wealth is not an easy or quick path that you can take without effort or sacrifice. It is a challenging and rewarding path that requires commitment and discipline. It is a complex and nuanced path that involves trade-offs and dilemmas. It is a paradoxical and contradictory path that embraces both abundance and simplicity, both freedom and responsibility, both self-interest and altruism. The wisdom of wealth is not a guarantee or promise that you will always be happy or successful. It is a possibility or opportunity that you can create or seize. It is a risk or adventure that you can take or avoid.

The wisdom of wealth is not an end or goal in itself, but a means or tool to achieve something greater and more meaningful. It is not an ultimate value or virtue, but a relative and instrumental value. It is not an intrinsic or inherent good, but a contingent and conditional good. The wisdom of wealth is not what defines or determines who you are or what you are worth as a human being. It is what enables or enhances what you can do or be as a human being.

In this chapter, we will explore some of the key principles of the wisdom of wealth, such as:

- **Finding your why:** How to discover your true purpose and passion in life
- **Living by your values:** How to align your actions with your core beliefs and principles
- **Creating your vision:** How to design your ideal life and set meaningful goals
- **Enjoying the journey:** How to appreciate the process and celebrate the progress
- **Balancing work and life:** How to manage your time and energy effectively

69

- **Impacting others**: How to use your wealth to make a positive difference in the world
- **Giving back**: How to share your wealth with others who need it more
- **Living authentically**: How to be yourself and express your uniqueness
- **Living creatively**: How to unleash your potential and pursue your passions
- **Living generously**: How to be grateful and generous with what you have

Finding your why: How to discover your true purpose and passion in life

One of the most important questions you can ask yourself is: Why do I exist? What is the reason for my being here? What is the unique contribution that I can make to the world? Finding your why is not easy, but it is essential for living a fulfilling and meaningful life. Your why is your ultimate motivation, your driving force, your reason to get up in the morning. Your why is what gives you direction, clarity, and focus. Your why is what inspires you and others.

How can you find your why? There are many ways to approach this question, but one of the most effective methods is to use the following three steps:

1) **Reflect on your past.** Think about the moments in your life when you felt most alive, most joyful, most fulfilled. What were you doing? Who were you with? What were you passionate about? What were the common themes or patterns that emerged from these experiences?

2) **Explore your present.** Think about the activities, people, causes, or topics that you are currently interested in, curious about, or excited by. What are you drawn to? What are you good at? What are you learning? What are the challenges or problems that you want to solve?

3) **Envision your future.** Think about the impact that you want to have on the world, the legacy that you want to leave behind, the difference that you want to make. What are your dreams? What are your aspirations? What are your values?

By combining these three perspectives, you can start to identify your why, your true purpose and passion in life. You can then use this as a guide for making decisions, setting goals, and choosing actions that align with your why.

70

Living by your values: How to align your actions with your core beliefs and principles

Living by your values: How to align your actions with your core beliefs and principles

Values are the fundamental beliefs that guide our behavior and choices. They are the standards that we use to evaluate what is important, what is right, what is wrong, what is good, what is bad. Values are the essence of who we are and what we stand for. They reflect our identity, our character, our personality.

Living by our values means acting in accordance with our core beliefs and principles, even when it is difficult, inconvenient, or unpopular. Living by our values means being authentic, consistent, and trustworthy. Living by our values means being true to ourselves and honoring our integrity.

How can we live by our values? Here are some tips to help us align our actions with our core beliefs and principles:

1) **Identify your values.** Make a list of the values that matter most to you, such as honesty, respect, compassion, courage, etc. You can use online tools or quizzes to help you with this process, or you can simply brainstorm on your own.

2) **Prioritize your values.** Rank your values in order of importance to you, from highest to lowest. You may have many values, but some may be more essential or fundamental than others. You may also have some conflicting or competing values that need to be resolved or balanced.

3) **Evaluate your actions.** Compare your current behavior and choices with your values. Are they aligned or misaligned? Are they congruent or incongruent? Are they supportive or detrimental? Identify any gaps or discrepancies between what you say and what you do.

4) **Adjust your actions.** If you find any areas where your actions do not match your values, take steps to correct them. Make a plan to change your habits, routines, or strategies to better reflect your values. Seek feedback, support, or accountability from others who share your values or who can help you stay on track.

71

By following these steps, you can live by your values and align your actions with your core beliefs and principles.

Creating your vision: How to design your ideal life and set meaningful goals

A vision is a clear and compelling picture of what you want your life to look like in the future. It is a description of your desired outcomes, results, or achievements in various areas of your life, such as personal, professional, social, spiritual, etc. A vision is a source of inspiration, motivation, and direction for your life.

Creating your vision means designing your ideal life and setting meaningful goals that will help you realize your vision. Creating your vision means imagining the best possible scenario for yourself and expressing it in a positive, specific, and realistic way.

How can you create your vision? Here are some steps to help you design your ideal life and set meaningful goals:

1) **Dream big.** Allow yourself to explore your deepest desires, your highest aspirations, your wildest fantasies. Don't limit yourself by fear, doubt, or practicality. Think about what you really want, not what you think you should want, or what others want for you.

2) **Write it down.** Put your vision into words, using the present tense, as if you have already achieved it. Use vivid, descriptive, and emotional language to make your vision as clear and compelling as possible. You can also use images, drawings, or collages to illustrate your vision visually.

3) **Break it down.** Divide your vision into smaller, more manageable parts, such as categories, areas, or domains of your life. For example, you can have a vision for your health, your career, your relationships, your hobbies, etc. Then, for each part, set specific, measurable, achievable, relevant, and time-bound (SMART) goals that will help you move closer to your vision.

4) **Take action.** Start working towards your goals, one step at a time. Create a plan of action that outlines the tasks, resources, and deadlines that you need to accomplish your goals. Monitor your progress and celebrate your achievements along the way. Adjust your plan as needed, based on feedback, results, or changes in circumstances.

72

By following these steps, you can create your vision and design your ideal life and set meaningful goals.

Enjoying the journey: How to appreciate the process and celebrate the progress

Many people focus so much on the destination that they forget to enjoy the journey. They are so obsessed with reaching their goals that they neglect to appreciate the process and celebrate the progress. They are so impatient for the future that they miss out on the present. They are so dissatisfied with what they have that they overlook what they have achieved.

This is a mistake, because enjoying the journey is not only more fun, but also more effective. Enjoying the journey means being grateful for what you have, being mindful of what you do, being optimistic about what you can, and being proud of what you did. Enjoying the journey means savoring the moments, learning the lessons, overcoming the challenges, and acknowledging the successes. Enjoying the journey means finding joy, meaning, and fulfillment in the process and progress of your life.

How can you enjoy the journey? Here are some ways to appreciate the process and celebrate the progress:

1) **Be present.** Pay attention to what is happening right now, rather than worrying about what might happen later or regretting what happened before. Focus on the task at hand, rather than multitasking or distracting yourself. Notice the details, sensations, emotions, and thoughts that arise in each moment. Practice mindfulness techniques, such as meditation, breathing, or journaling, to help you stay in the present moment.

2) **Be grateful.** Express gratitude for what you have, rather than complaining about what you lack. Appreciate the people, opportunities, resources, and experiences that you have in your life. Recognize the positive aspects, benefits, and advantages of your situation. Write down or say out loud what you are thankful for every day. Show appreciation to others who have helped or supported you along the way.

3) **Be optimistic.** Adopt a positive attitude towards what you can do, rather than a negative one towards what you can't do. Look for the possibilities, solutions, and opportunities in every situation. Expect good things to happen, rather than bad things. Believe in yourself and your abilities, rather

73

than doubting or criticizing yourself. Use affirmations, visualization, or self-talk to boost your confidence and motivation.

4) **Be proud.** Acknowledge what you did, rather than ignoring or minimizing it. Celebrate your achievements, big or small, rather than dismissing or downplaying them. Reward yourself for your efforts, hard work, and perseverance. Share your accomplishments with others who care about you and who will cheer for you. Reflect on how far you have come, how much you have grown, and how much you have learned.

By following these ways, you can enjoy the journey and appreciate the process and celebrate the progress of your life.

Balancing work and life: How to manage your time and energy effectively

Balancing work and life is a challenge that many people face, especially those who have achieved a high level of success and wealth. It can be tempting to devote all your time and energy to your work, but this can lead to burnout, stress, and dissatisfaction. To avoid these negative outcomes, you need to find a way to balance your work and life, and enjoy both aspects of your existence.

One way to balance work and life is to set clear boundaries and priorities. You need to decide what is important to you, and what you are willing to compromise on. For example, you may decide that you will not work on weekends, or that you will limit your work hours to a certain number per day. You may also decide that you will spend quality time with your family, friends, or hobbies every week. By setting these boundaries and priorities, you can ensure that you have enough time and energy for both work and life.

Another way to balance work and life is to delegate and outsource tasks that are not essential or enjoyable for you. You may have a lot of responsibilities and obligations, but you do not have to do everything yourself. You can hire professionals, assistants, or consultants to help you with tasks that are tedious, time-consuming, or stressful. For example, you may hire a financial planner, a personal chef, a housekeeper, or a personal trainer. By delegating and outsourcing these tasks, you can free up your time and energy for more important or rewarding activities.

A third way to balance work and life is to practice self-care and wellness. You need to take care of yourself physically, mentally, and emotionally, in order to perform well at work and enjoy life. You can do this by eating well, exercising regularly, sleeping enough, meditating, relaxing, or doing anything that makes you happy and

74

healthy. By practicing self-care and wellness, you can boost your mood, energy, productivity, and creativity.

Balancing work and life is not easy, but it is possible and beneficial. By following these tips, you can manage your time and energy effectively, and achieve a fulfilling and harmonious existence.

Impacting others: How to use your wealth to make a positive difference in the world

Impacting others is a noble goal that many wealthy people aspire to. You may have worked hard to earn your wealth, but you may also want to use it to make a positive difference in the world. You may want to help others who are less fortunate than you, or support causes that are important to you. You may want to leave a legacy that will inspire future generations. How can you do this?

One way to impact others is to donate your money to charities or organizations that align with your values and vision. You can research the causes that you care about, and find reputable and effective organizations that are working on them. You can then donate as much as you can afford, either as a one-time gift or as a recurring donation. You can also encourage others to donate as well, by matching their contributions or creating fundraising campaigns. By donating your money, you can support the work of these organizations and help them achieve their goals.

Another way to impact others is to invest your money in social enterprises or impact funds that aim to create positive social or environmental change. You can look for businesses or funds that have a clear mission and vision, and that measure their impact using reliable indicators. You can then invest as much as you can afford in these businesses or funds, either as equity or debt. You can also mentor or advise these businesses or funds, by sharing your expertise or network. By investing your money, you can help these businesses or funds grow and scale their impact.

A third way to impact others is to create your own foundation or organization that focuses on a specific issue or area that you are passionate about. You can define your mission and vision, and set your goals and strategies. You can then hire staff or volunteers who share your passion and values. You can also partner with other foundations or organizations that have similar objectives or complementary skills. By creating your own foundation or organization, you can lead the change that you want to see in the world.

Impacting others is not only a generous act but also a rewarding one. By following these tips, you can use your wealth to make a positive difference in the world.

Giving back: How to share your wealth with others who need it more

Giving back is a virtue that many wealthy people practice. You may have accumulated a lot of wealth through your work or inheritance, but you may also feel a sense of gratitude and responsibility towards others who have less than you. You may want to share your wealth with others who need it more than you do, either locally or globally. You may want to improve their lives and opportunities in some way. How can you do this?

One way to give back is to volunteer your time and skills to causes or organizations that serve the needy or disadvantaged. You can find opportunities that match your interests and abilities, such as teaching children, mentoring entrepreneurs, building houses, providing medical care, or protecting the environment. You can then commit as much time as you can spare, either regularly or occasionally. You can also recruit others to join you, by creating or joining volunteer groups or networks. By volunteering your time and skills, you can make a direct and personal impact on others.

Another way to give back is to sponsor individuals or groups who have potential but lack resources or opportunities. You can identify people or groups who have talent, passion, or ambition, but face barriers or challenges that prevent them from achieving their goals. You can then sponsor them financially or otherwise, by providing scholarships, grants, loans, equipment, training, or mentorship. You can also follow up and support them throughout their journey, by giving feedback, advice, or encouragement. By sponsoring individuals or groups, you can empower them to pursue their dreams and succeed.

A third way to give back is to advocate for causes or issues that affect the well-being or rights of others. You can use your voice, influence, or platform to raise awareness, educate, or persuade others about the causes or issues that you care about. You can also use your connections, networks, or resources to lobby, campaign, or mobilize others to take action or demand change. You can also join or support movements or coalitions that share your vision and values. By advocating for causes or issues, you can amplify your impact and inspire others to join you.

Giving back is not only a moral duty but also a joyful experience. By following these tips, you can share your wealth with others who need it more than you do.

76

Living authentically: How to be yourself and express your uniqueness

Living authentically means being true to yourself and expressing your uniqueness. It means not conforming to the expectations or norms of others, but rather following your own values, interests and passions. Living authentically can help you feel more confident, fulfilled and free. Some ways to live authentically are:

- **Identify your core values and align your actions with them.** For example, if you value honesty, integrity and respect, you can act accordingly in your personal and professional relationships. You can also communicate your values to others and stand up for what you believe in.

- **Explore your interests and hobbies and pursue them with enthusiasm.** For example, if you love music, art or sports, you can dedicate time and energy to practice, learn and improve your skills. You can also join communities or groups that share your interests and hobbies.

- **Express your opinions and feelings honestly and respectfully.** For example, if you have a different perspective or preference than someone else, you can share it without being afraid of judgment or rejection. You can also listen to others' opinions and feelings with an open mind and empathy.

- **Celebrate your strengths and embrace your weaknesses.** For example, if you are good at writing, speaking or organizing, you can use these strengths to contribute to your goals or causes. You can also acknowledge your weaknesses and seek help or feedback to overcome them.

- **Accept yourself as you are and avoid comparing yourself to others.** For example, if you have a unique personality, appearance or style, you can embrace it and express it without trying to fit in or please others. You can also appreciate the diversity and uniqueness of others without feeling inferior or superior.

Living creatively: How to unleash your potential and pursue your passions

Living creatively means unleashing your potential and pursuing your passions. It means not settling for the status quo, but rather seeking new challenges, opportunities and experiences. Living creatively can help you feel more inspired, motivated and alive. Some ways to live creatively are:

- **Set goals and work towards them with passion and perseverance.** For example, if you have a dream or a vision for your future, you can break it down into smaller steps and work on them every day. You can also track your progress and celebrate your achievements.

- **Learn new skills and expand your knowledge.** For example, if you are curious about a topic or a field, you can enroll in a course, read a book or watch a video to learn more about it. You can also apply what you learn in practical or creative ways.

- **Try new things and experiment with different approaches.** For example, if you are bored or stuck in a routine, you can try something new or different that challenges you or sparks your interest. You can also experiment with different methods or tools to solve problems or create something new.

- **Use your imagination and creativity to solve problems or create something new.** For example, if you face a problem or an obstacle, you can use your imagination and creativity to find a solution or an alternative. You can also use your imagination and creativity to create something original or innovative that expresses your ideas or emotions.

- **Seek feedback and learn from your mistakes.** For example, if you want to improve your performance or output, you can seek feedback from others who have more experience or expertise than you. You can also learn from your mistakes and failures and use them as opportunities to grow.

Living generously: How to be grateful and generous with what you have

Living generously means being grateful and generous with what you have. It means not taking things for granted, but rather appreciating the abundance and beauty of life. Living generously can help you feel more connected, compassionate and joyful. Some ways to live generously are:

- **Express gratitude for the people, things and experiences in your life.** For example, if you have supportive family members, friends or colleagues, you can thank them for their presence and help in your life. You can also express gratitude for the things that make your life easier or more enjoyable, such as food, water, shelter, health, technology or nature.

78

- **Share your time, talents and resources with others who need them.** For example, if you have spare time, skills or money that you can offer to others who are less fortunate than you, you can do so through volunteering, donating or mentoring. You can also share your knowledge, wisdom or advice with others who seek them.

- **Volunteer for a cause that matters to you or help someone in need.** For example, if you care about a social or environmental issue that affects the world or your community, you can volunteer for an organization that works on that issue. You can also help someone in need by offering a hand, a hug or a listening ear.

- **Compliment, encourage and support others.** For example, if you notice something positive about someone else's personality, appearance or work, you can compliment them sincerely and genuinely. You can also encourage and support others who are pursuing their goals or facing difficulties.

- **Practice kindness and forgiveness towards yourself and others.** For example, if you make a mistake or hurt someone, you can be kind and forgiving towards yourself and apologize sincerely. You can also be kind and forgiving towards others who make mistakes or hurt you and accept their apologies.

By applying these principles to your life, you will be able to use your wealth wisely and well. You will be able to achieve not only financial success, but also personal fulfillment and happiness. You will be able to live not only a rich life, but also a meaningful life. You will be able to experience not only the power of wealth, but also the wisdom of wealth.

CHAPTER 19: The Art of Wealth

You have learned a lot about wealth in this book. You have learned what wealth is, why it matters, how to create it, how to manage it, how to multiply it, how to protect it, how to use it, how to enjoy it, and how to pass it on. You have learned the concepts, the principles, the methods, the techniques, the systems, and the secrets of wealth. You have learned the mindset, the habits, the skills, the strategies, the tools, and the ethics of wealth. You have learned the psychology, the relationships, the lifestyle, the legacy, and the future of wealth.

But there is one more thing you need to learn about wealth. And that is the art of wealth.

What is the art of wealth? It is the ability to express yourself through your wealth. It is the ability to create something beautiful, meaningful, and unique with your wealth. It is the ability to use your wealth as a medium of communication, expression, and contribution. It is the ability to make your wealth a reflection of who you are, what you value, and what you stand for.

The art of wealth is not about how much money you have or what you own. It is about how you use your money and what you create with it. It is about how you make your money work for you and for others. It is about how you make your money a source of joy and fulfillment for yourself and for others.

The art of wealth is not something that can be taught or learned in a book. It is something that can only be discovered and developed by yourself. It is something that requires creativity, imagination, intuition, and inspiration. It is something that requires passion, purpose, vision, and mission. It is something that requires courage, confidence, authenticity, and integrity.

80

The art of wealth is not something that can be measured or quantified by numbers or statistics. It is something that can only be felt and appreciated by yourself and by others. It is something that can only be expressed and shared by yourself and by others. It is something that can only be admired and respected by yourself and by others.

The art of wealth is not something that can be copied or duplicated by others. It is something that can only be created and innovated by yourself. It is something that can only be original and unique to yourself. It is something that can only be personal and meaningful to yourself.

The art of wealth is not something that can be achieved or accomplished by following a formula or a recipe. It is something that can only be experienced and enjoyed by following your heart and your soul. It is something that can only be realized and manifested by following your dreams and your destiny.

The art of wealth is not something that can be defined or explained by words or concepts. It is something that can only be shown and demonstrated by actions and results. It is something that can only be lived and embodied by examples and models.

The art of wealth is not something that can be mastered or perfected by anyone. It is something that can only be practiced and improved by yourself. It is something that can only be challenged and tested by yourself. It is something that can only be grown and evolved by yourself.

The art of wealth is not something that can be finished or completed by anyone. It is something that can only be started and continued by yourself. It is something that can only be explored and expanded by yourself. It is something that can only be sustained and maintained by yourself.

The art of wealth is not something that can be given or taken by anyone. It is something that can only be earned and deserved by yourself. It is something that can only be shared and contributed by yourself. It is something that can only be appreciated and celebrated by yourself.

The art of wealth is not a destination or a goal. It is a journey or a process. It is not a result or an outcome. It is an experience or a state of being. It is not a product or a service. It is a creation or a gift.

81

CHAPTER 20: The Challenge of Wealth

Wealth is often seen as a desirable goal in life, but it also poses many challenges and risks. Wealth can bring happiness, comfort, security, and opportunities, but it can also cause stress, anxiety, isolation, and corruption. In this chapter, we will explore some of the psychological, social, and ethical aspects of wealth and how to cope with them.

One of the main psychological challenges of wealth is the paradox of choice. Having more money means having more options and possibilities, but it also means having more decisions and trade-offs. Research has shown that too much choice can lead to dissatisfaction, regret, and paralysis. For example, a wealthy person may struggle to choose among hundreds of vacation destinations, while a poor person may be happy with any opportunity to travel. To overcome this challenge, wealthy people need to learn how to simplify their choices, prioritize their values, and accept their limitations.

Another psychological challenge of wealth is the hedonic treadmill. This is the tendency for people to adapt to their circumstances and return to their baseline level of happiness, regardless of positive or negative changes. For example, a wealthy person may experience a temporary boost in happiness after buying a new car, but soon get used to it and want something better. This can lead to a cycle of dissatisfaction and consumerism, where wealth becomes a source of stress rather than joy. To overcome this challenge, wealthy people need to practice gratitude, generosity, and mindfulness, and focus on the intrinsic rather than extrinsic rewards of their activities.

A third psychological challenge of wealth is the loss of meaning and purpose. Having more money can make life easier, but it can also make it less meaningful and fulfilling. For example, a wealthy person may not have to work for a living, but may

82

also lose the sense of achievement and contribution that work can provide. Similarly, a wealthy person may have more leisure time, but may also feel bored and restless without any challenges or goals. To overcome this challenge, wealthy people need to find ways to use their wealth for a greater good, such as supporting causes they care about, helping others in need, or creating something valuable for society.

Besides the psychological challenges, wealth also poses social challenges. One of the main social challenges of wealth is the difficulty of maintaining authentic relationships. Wealth can create barriers between people, such as envy, resentment, mistrust, or exploitation. For example, a wealthy person may wonder if their friends and partners like them for who they are or for what they have. Alternatively, a wealthy person may feel lonely and isolated because they have few peers who can relate to their problems and experiences. To overcome this challenge, wealthy people need to cultivate genuine connections with others based on mutual respect, honesty, and compassion.

Another social challenge of wealth is the responsibility of stewardship. Wealth can give people power and influence over others, but it also comes with accountability and expectations. For example, a wealthy person may have to manage their assets wisely, pay their taxes fairly, and contribute to society generously. Alternatively, a wealthy person may face criticism or backlash if they misuse their wealth for selfish or harmful purposes. To overcome this challenge,
wealthy people need to develop ethical principles and practices that guide their decisions and actions regarding their wealth.

A final social challenge of wealth is the impact on the environment. Wealth can enable people to consume more resources and produce more waste than the average person. For example, a wealthy person may travel frequently by plane or car, use more electricity and water at home or work, or buy more products that require energy and materials to produce. This can have negative consequences for the planet's health and sustainability. To overcome this challenge,
wealthy people need to adopt eco-friendly habits and lifestyles that reduce their environmental footprint and support green initiatives.

In summary, wealth is not only a blessing but also a challenge. Wealth can bring many benefits but also many problems for individuals and society. Wealthy people need to be aware of these challenges and learn how to cope with them effectively.

CONCLUSION

You have reached the end of this book, but not the end of your journey to wealth. In this book, you have learned the formula of wealth, which is based on four pillars: mindset, habits, skills and strategies. You have also discovered the tools, risks, ethics, psychology, relationships, lifestyle, legacy, future, secrets, myths, opportunities, wisdom and art of wealth. These are the elements that make up the rich and fulfilling life that you deserve.

But knowing the formula of wealth is not enough. You have to apply it in your daily life. You have to take action and implement what you have learned. You have to practice the principles and follow the examples of successful people. You have to overcome your fears and doubts and face the challenges and obstacles that may come your way. You have to be persistent and consistent in your pursuit of wealth.

Wealth is not a destination, but a process. It is not a fixed amount of money, but a state of mind. It is not a privilege, but a responsibility. It is not a gift, but a reward. It is not a luck, but a choice. It is not a fantasy, but a reality.

You have the power to create, manage and multiply your money. You have the potential to achieve your financial goals and dreams. You have the opportunity to make a positive impact on yourself, your family, your community and the world. You have the responsibility to use your wealth wisely and ethically. You have the wisdom to enjoy your wealth and share it with others. You have the art to live a wealthy life.

This book is not the end, but the beginning of your journey to wealth. I hope you have found it valuable and inspiring. I hope you will use it as a guide and a reference in your quest for wealth. I hope you will share it with others who may benefit from it. I hope you will keep learning and growing as a person and as a wealth creator.

Thank you for reading this book. I wish you all the best in your journey to wealth.